DISPATCHES
FROM
MAINE

Books by John Gould
(so far)

New England Town Meeting
Pre-natal Care for Fathers
Farmer Takes a Wife
The House That Jacob Built
And One to Grow On
Neither Hay Nor Grass
Monstrous Depravity
The Parables of Peter Partout
You Should Start Sooner
Last One In
Europe on Saturday Night
The Jonesport Raffle
Twelve Grindstones
The Shag Bag
Glass Eyes by the Bottle
This Trifling Distinction
Next Time Around
No Other Place
Stitch in Time
The Wines of Pentagoët
Old Hundredth
There Goes Maine!
Funny About That
It Is Not Now
Dispatches from Maine

With Lillian Ross
Maine Lingo

With F. Wenderoth Saunders
The Fastest Hound Dog in the State of Maine

DISPATCHES
FROM
MAINE

1942–1992

JOHN GOULD

W. W. Norton & Company
New York   *London*

Printed in the United States of America
We are grateful to the *Christian Science Monitor* for their permission to reprint
each of the pieces included herein, which originally appeared as columns in
their publication.
First Edition
This text of this book is composed in 10/13 Palatino.
Composition and manufacturing by the Maple Vail Book Manufacturing Group

Library of Congress Cataloging-in-Publication Data
Gould, John, 1908–
Dispatches from Maine : 1942–1992 / John Gould.
p. cm.
1. Maine—Social life and customs. I. Title.
F19.G68 1994
974.1—dc20   93-33215

ISBN 0-393-03624-3
W. W. Norton & Company, Inc., 500 Fifth Avenue, New York, N.Y. 10110
W. W. Norton & Company Ltd., 10 Coptic Street, London WC1A 1PU
1 2 3 4 5 6 7 8 9 0

Erwin Dain Canham
1904–1982

My father and Vincent Canham were schoolday chums, and Vincent grew up to be farm editor of the Lewiston, Maine, newspapers—as well as the father of Erwin Dain Canham. Erwin's mother was one of the Gowell girls, of whom Aunt Cora was my neighbor at Lisbon Falls. Erwin had been editor of the *Christian Science Monitor* about a year when I, a hopeful young man, mailed him a bundle of light essays with the notion they might accentuate the otherwise high quality journalism of his illustrious newspaper. His reply was favorable, and on October 21, 1942, the first of fifty years of consecutive weekly dispatches was printed. I think in all I saw Erwin Canham four times; the United States Postal Service made it unnecessary to visit the publishing house. In forty years I had but four letters from him. Now that I'm rounding out my fifty years with the paper he served so long so well, I write his name on this page because it belongs here.

J. G.

Friendship, Maine, 1992

Contents

Peter Partout's Page

Dear Mr. Editor: I've lived pretty-much next-door to this Gould boy a long time and I didn't realize that he's been at it all these years. Makes me feel proud to know him, and I'm going to read this book just as soon as the library gets a copy.

(Signed) Peter Partout—Peppermint Corner, Maine

Readers Write

6 June 1971

To the *Christian Science Monitor:*

While spending a year stationed in remote Alaska I have discovered one more outstanding feature of the *Monitor* which I
consider not only a journalistic gem but also a great public service—John Gould's "Dispatch from the Farm." Besides provid-
ing ever-needed humor, the column should serve as a reminder
to us all that civilization and progress should never be taken at
face value. I think it is high time that either the Monitor or Mr.
Gould himself made available a volume of selected dispatches,
and I will be happy to purchase the first copy! Won't you please
share this letter with Mr. Gould?

Lt. Ethan Hirsch

Foreword

"We don't write books in Maine," John Gould once wrote, "We *live* books. We go hunting and fishing, we tend out on Grange meetings, we socialize as time permits, and after we've done enough living in Maine the pile is big enough and we send it to a publisher."

John Gould has been living his way onto the pages of *The Christian Science Monitor* for more than half a century. This book is a selection of his columns from 1942 to 1992: his weekly "Dispatch from the Farm" that appeared for many years on the Editorial Page and his Friday essays that now are published on the Home Forum Page.

The Gould family homes in Freeport, Lisbon Falls, and Friendship, Maine, have been the backdrop for many a column. Readers arrived late to school with young John (he had been feeding his hens), visited the sugar house and learned carpentry with John's small daughter and son, and picnicked with his grandchildren when they appeared on the scene. John's "favorite wife," Dorothy, has been a constant through the years, as has a colorful parade of lobstermen, loggers, country schoolteachers, and hardworking farm wives.

The characters of Gould's world live with a laconic humor that is typical of Maine. Sometimes, a reader may know his leg is being tugged at, but at others he may wonder with a smile whether a tall tale is being spun around him. "I don't think there's any such thing as fiction," Gould once said in a *Monitor* interview. "Writing's got to come from something that's happened to you or somebody else. . . . There's got to be a smack of realism and factualism to back me up and make the writing plausible. There has to be enough there to make the reader relate to it."

And for decades, readers *have* related. They have written him letters by the droves, and many have even found their way to his home in hopes of shaking his hand. They have told him that his stories remind them of their grandmothers' kitchens in Missouri or South Carolina—that his columns speak of the comfort and warmth of home.

In the summer of 1992, as the fiftieth anniversary of the publication of John Gould's first *Monitor* column approached, the paper invited readers to send congratulations and to share their thoughts about his writing. By October 21, the anniversary, more than 1,400 letters and postcards had arrived from all over the world. One in particular, from Surrey, England, spoke for many and also related an experience that captures the essence of a Gould column:

> *Dear Mr. Gould,*
>
> *How remarkable that we should be about to congratulate you on your 50th anniversary with The Christian Science Monitor.*
>
> *To put it as simply and briefly as possible— my Fridays would not be complete without your special message from Friendship, Maine. It brings humour and interest to my day, and I often share your contribution with my whole office.*
>
> *Do you remember I wrote to you about a young soldier [serving in Vietnam whom] I met when he was on R and R in Bangkok? I met him one morning by the hotel pool, and he was clearly sad and homesick. I asked where he came from, and he said Maine. I asked him if he knew Lisbon Falls, and he said [it] was just a few miles down the road from his own*

town. He wouldn't believe me when I told him that I read
a weekly article in a daily newspaper from there.
It just so happened that there was a Friday Monitor
in the paper rack in that hotel's lobby, and I
went in and got it and gave it to him.

You can't imagine the joy that article gave
to that young soldier so many miles from home. Not
just the content, but the fact that it came from
Lisbon Falls. You cured him of homesickness, and
it was a privilege for me to be a small part of
that little episode.

Just a small example of the goodness and joy
your articles have spread around the world.

John L. Miller

An old friend, a faithful companion, a purveyor of soft chuck-
les. These were the words readers used to describe John Gould.
As this book is published, the staff and readers of the *Monitor*
join in saluting John's enduring humor and wit, the mastery
of his craft, and the immense contribution he has made to our
newspaper over the last 51 years.

Alice M. Hummer
Editor, The Home Forum Page
The Christian Science Monitor
Boston
October 1993

1942
Buck-Saws and Christmas Trees

T here is reason to believe that, if the sun came up with a
derby hat on some morning, most of my neighbors would
not look twice, and would hardly mention it to their wives when
they came up from the barns to breakfast. Our rural community
has been conditioned by several generations of whimsical folk
who seem to have had a lot of fun doing things that were not a
bit different from putting a bowler on Old Sol.

This facet of life on the Ridge has never been satisfactorily
explained beyond our borders, possibly because we are now
accustomed to it and seldom feel the need of explaining. It is
true that our explanations are always as queer to strangers as
the original deed, and that naturally complicates matters.

I remember when someone looked up at Wadell's one morning and discovered that Chris Wadell had painted his silo with
red, white, and blue stripes, making the structure look something like a huge barber pole. The silo sat on top of the hill, and
could be seen to the limits of the horizon when it was merely a
subdued weather color, but now it could be heard as well as
seen. Not a man in the neighborhood commented on this
improvement, and it is likely Chris never expected them to. It is
said that a man from Worcester, who was driving through on
business, once drove in and asked Chris why he painted his silo
that way.

Chris said it was to preserve the wood.

I suppose I was guilty of some such foolishness when I made my buck-saw out of black walnut. Odd jobs that had been saved for a rainy day were being disposed of, and I came to the task of making a buck-saw frame. I stood up on a barrel and poked around 'mid the bits of scrap lumber that were being seasoned over the beams. I had some ash, but thought it would cut to waste, and hesitated to use oak because buck-saws sometimes get left out in the rain, and oak will soak water like a lobster trap. I turned over a board, and found a lovely piece of black walnut. I probably originally intended to use it for a silver chest, a stand, or some similar bit of beauty. But it was quickly fashioned into a buck-saw frame, and it was a grand piece of wood to work. When I had it strung together, and filed the saw, it was still raining; so I inlaid the handle with some cherry and basswood, and carved rosettes at the top. How far I might have gone, had supper not interfered, is anyone's guess.

I was sawing wood with it a few nights later when Charlie Little wandered in to see if I wanted to buy a shoat. I laid the saw down to put another stick on the saw-horse, and Charlie picked up my buck-saw and scrutinized it. He ran his leathery thumb over the inlay, rubbed the walnut against the back of his hand, plucked a thumb-nail across a saw-tooth to test the filing, and then reached over and sawed off a stick. He handed the saw to me without comment, which indicated that the matter had his approval, if not his understanding.

But I think it did have his complete understanding, for they tell me about the time Charlie set up a Christmas tree in August. He was swamping out a road back in the woods, and came across a young fir that had a perfect shape. The limbs were evenly spaced, each had an identical amount of needles, and the top tapered off with rare beauty. Charlie had to slice it down, because it was right in the middle of his road, but he thought it was a shame to let it go to waste simply because it wasn't December.

So he brought it to the house, fashioned a standard for it, and put it up on the front piazza ablaze with lights, festooned with strings of popcorn, and adorned with a number of gaily wrapped bundles that his wife fixed. It was a vision, and the family would sit out on the piazza in the cool of the evening and enjoy it. Neighbors who dropped in to sit would greet the Littles with, "Merry Christmas!" but that's about all the comment there was. . . .

My grandfather used to plant his flower garden along with his vegetables. Gladioli mingled with carrots; dahlias were hung with pole beans; asters were revealed when the frost wilted pumpkins and squash; and nasturtiums entwined with the cucumbers. I doubt if anyone in town ever asked him why he, as if he couldn't tell the difference, thus mixed up his seed. It isn't usual, certainly. Had you asked him, he would have said he spent most of the summer among his garden sass, and that was where he had to have his flowers if he were to enjoy them. But nobody on the Ridge ever gave the hodgepodge second thought. Time and again there has been evidence that our neighbors are willing to indulge each other in whimsey.

I have really wondered, lately, if this tolerance isn't a remote desideratum among other people. Are we peculiar in our private belief that a man's own inclination is to be indulged? Haven't other people taken too much stock in the belief that all activity must be rationalized—and that the reasons ought to be sensible? I mean, apparently sensible to others? Hasn't conformity to rules of behavior taken a lot of snap out of life? Who dares to paint his steps yellow, simply because he likes yellow? What housewife dares to hang the wash on the front lawn? It just simply isn't done—is it?

Well, I suppose I've got the only inlaid black walnut buck-saw in the world.

1942
Fame Is Spelled in Lower Case

As I headed up a rivet on the mowing machine the other day, it occurred to me that everlasting fame does not necessarily consist of being famous forever. If the apparent redundancy of the foregoing sentence bothers you, perhaps you will then assist me in proving my point by telling all you know about Mr. Pitman.

Now that you have revealed such utter ignorance of that worthy man, let me add that every farmer in the United States can tell you that the pitman rod on a mowing machine is what makes the scythe skitter in the cutter-bar—the device that converts a rotary motion to a lateral to-and-fro. Even the dictionary will assist you by saying that the pitman is a rod connecting a crank pin with a piston. Actually, it is a wooden rod (that breaks two or three times during the mowing season) without which a mowing machine would be useless. Likewise, as every dweller along mid-Western rivers knows, it is the bar that drives the great stern paddle wheels.

It was invented, as far as recollection serves, by a Mr. Pitman. But where are the snows of yesteryear? Where is Mr. Pitman? Who was he? Where did he live? Only stubborn research would reveal all that—and yet his name is annually on the tongues of a million farmers. *Sic transit gloria mundi.*

From musing thus, it was only a step to a consideration of Mr. McAdam, whose highways have lately been superseded by Mr.

Tarvia and Mr. Bituminous-Asphalt. We knock the capital letters from his name, and burn four gallons a week on his roads without the faintest notion of his name and career. No doubt the reference books behind me here would tell a lot about the gentleman, but a world familiar with macadam roads isn't much concerned with the life of Mr. McAdam.

No doubt it is the same with Mr. Watt, who lives forever on the electric light statements. We all remember the steaming tea-kettle story—but what else? I do recall that Mr. Morris left some literature in addition to an adjustable armchair, but I rather guess the world suspects he was really two different men. A name that lives forever isn't always a guarantee of men's remembrance.

Finally, take Mr. Peavey. He invented a device for rolling logs, the fame of which spread from Bangor, Maine, throughout the world. Mr. Peavey, as far as most of us are concerned, is one with Nineveh and Tyre. But with a peavey we move our logs, and the name will live as long as men take timber to a mill.

It is no doubt in the minds of many of us to leave our footprints on the sands of time. But Mr. Pitman and Mr. Peavey and others of that memorably-forgotten band caution us to be careful what boon we contribute to establish ourselves for posterity. When that man makes the better mousetrap, his name will no doubt go on and on and on. But it probably will be spelled with a small letter, even as we now are tempted to do with diesel engine and pullman car.

1943
Whistles Without Price

No doubt no belated remarks of mine will dim the mellowed fame of Benjamin Franklin, who once admonished us not to pay too much for our whistles. Mr. Franklin, of course, was a practical man, and he had a practical man's attitude toward whistles. He probably regarded a whistle as so much material, so much manufacturing time, so much ingenuity, and a bit of wind. Through this kind of inventory one would compute whistles as expensive at ten cents the gross, or in Franklin's time at not more than a shilling the shoal.

I am as much in love with practicality as the next one, but all in its proper place and at a convenient time. But according to my exceedingly impractical estimate of a whistle, I would not for anything share the sentiments of Mr. Franklin. I have just arrived at the whimsical conclusion that the world doesn't hold enough money to weigh off the kind of a whistle I made today. What this does to the reputation of Benjamin Franklin I care not one toot.

It is spring. The winter rye is growing by inches, and the pussy willows have turned to leaves. The first bob-o-link and the first oriole saluted us. One of the hens seemed to think of something and started clucking. The apple buds are tight pink clusters. It is whistle weather.

Once in a man's whole lifetime does the true and perfect whistle weather come. It is not contingent on the man's age— but on that of his son. Four-and-a-half seems to be a convenient age, with the spring at the morn and the Balm o' Gilead heavy in the air. Nobody says anything about whistles, of course, and at four-and-a-half the world holds so many surprises that amazement is an overworked and ever present expression.

To make a whistle properly, a man holds his son by the hand, and they walk out by the pond and watch the peepers scurry for the deep parts. It is carefully explained that peepers live in stone walls and such places all year, but have to lay their eggs in the water.

"Like hen's eggs, Daddy?"

And the walk goes on past the bee hives, where a few bees are flying in with pollen on their legs. It is an inspection tour— we find the first shoots of asparagus, the first leaves on the raspberries. We straighten a fence post and prop it with a rock, until we can really fix it.

"Can the cow jump that high?"

We find some ferns poking their fiddle-heads. We find a boxberry plum. As we look over the stone wall we see some violets, and a trillium.

"We'll pick some for Mummy on the way back."

A crow sees us coming and with a startled squawk drops behind a pine. Things are going nicely until four two-motored bombers roar over in what serves as an intrusion, and the lad calls victoriously, "Army Flash!" The planes are the only change in a scene that I saw at another man's hand once—it seemed long ago until this morning, but this morning it seemed hopefully recent. So recent that the two mornings became one, and somehow I was both father and son and knew just how each side of the dialog should proceed.

I knew at once that the next thing was to make a whistle. A willow shoot, a rolling cut with the small blade of the knife—a twist and off comes the bark. Small eyes are watching—but they can't see ahead some three decades or more when time will be right again for another whistle.

It doesn't take long. The smooth willow wood is wet in the mouth, and the bark slides back into place. All that is needed now is the puffed-out cheeks of a little boy, the resultant screech, and the sparkle of wonder in eyes that seldom have else than wonder when Daddy is around.

Because that whistle proves as nothing ever did that Daddy is the smartest and best and finest and grandest man in the whole world. For generations untold a willow whistle has been sager than Wisdom herself, and as I watch him and hear him blow his soul into each toot, I know it will always be so. And now we must go back to the house and show Mummy the whistle.

Mummy, of course, is delighted, and says, "Wasn't Daddy nice?" But Mummy is Mummy, and Mummies don't really understand things like men and boys and whistles. Like Benjamin Franklin, who was very practical, they couldn't ever know that once—no, twice—in a lifetime a whistle is beyond price.

1943
Molly Remembers the Day

The lane to the pasture runs along the line fence, past the raspberries and the high bush blueberries, past the tiled spring with the tumbler upside-down on the cover, and under the branches of the old Red Astrachan. Then it dodges under the low limbs of a white pine and you can't look back any more and see the barn. But you can look ahead up an aisle of pine needles and see blue sky over the four peeled-spruce bars at the gap. Usually the cows are there, eager to get to the barn for their grain and their squirt with fly spray.

Today, though, was the first the cows were out this spring, and we knew it would take a long walk through the woods to find them. They like to wander, when they first get out to grass, and during the winter they have forgotten the habit of coming home in the evening. Molly, the red one, has a bell, and wherever Molly goes the black one follows. Molly doesn't like the black one, probably on that account.

So we took down the bars, the lad and I, and stepped through into the pasture and stood still to listen. Over to one side the hylas were peeping in the wet place, and a mixed chorus of birds came up from the tall trees—but no bell. We walked on and on, away down through the woods to the lower field, and there was the bell and there were the cows. Molly looked up, dutifully came toward us and walked by on the way home. The black one danced around somewhat and then fell in behind.

But instead of going directly home, Molly turned off at the open spring in the hemlocks, skirted along the lower wall, and came up through the sugar place. She put her head into a clump of firs, pushed through them, and stopped on the other side to see if we were coming. The black one went around, but we pushed through and came out beside Molly and were glad we did.

"Gee-whillickers!" said the lad, "Gee-whillickers!"

The damp ground was carpeted with long-stemmed purple violets, a patch maybe 50 feet across rimmed with young firs, and so thick with blossoms we couldn't walk without stepping on them. Molly probably meant to take us there, to show the fine discovery she had made on her first day out—but she was slatting her head at flies and didn't say so. She stood, slatting and chewing, while we picked a bouquet, and the black one trotted around through the first and made out she was indignant.

When we had enough for the yellow bowl we called to Molly and she backed into the firs, swung around, and went directly up the hill and through the beeches in a straight line for the gap. The black one came along and we trailed them down and came out under the limbs of the pine. They went into the barn all right, and found their grain, and we fastened their chains for the night. When we went up to the house the lad carried the violets in both hands in front of him, and he stumbled on the doorsill but caught his balance just in time and stuck the flowers up at his mother.

"Here!" he said.

"Oh," said his mother, "what a lovely bouquet for Mother's Day. Such nice long stems! Aren't they lovely!"

"Is today Mother's Day?" he asked.

"No, dear, tomorrow is—didn't you know that?"

"Nope," he said, "but I guess Molly did."

1943
Oscar Was No Ordinary Bull

The other night, my city-bred bean pickers were sitting by the fireplace conducting a commando raid on a pan of Yellow Transparents, and we got to talking about farm bookkeeping. One thing led to another, and I told them about Oscar, the bull who telephoned to Cleveland. The story touched them deeply, and they urged me to prepare it for my next dispatch.

It came about this way: I was explaining how we arrive at some of our costs, and how farm accounts tumble over each other until the best of us are puzzled. For instance, the cost of maintaining a bull must be levied proportionately against the producing members of the dairy herd—yet figuring the maintenance expense of the old boy is far from easy. Take the telephone, I said, the amount of the bill must be prorated and the bull must stand his share.

"Ha-ha," laughed Madeline. "Who ever heard of a bull using a telephone?"

So I told them about Oscar. Oscar was by no means an ordinary bull, but had several unusual escapades to his credit. Some of them were undoubtedly apocryphal, but mostly they were like the time he charged the Guiding Star Ladies' Club and ate 127 cream cheese and olive sandwiches. The time he telephoned Aunt Hulda in Cleveland stands out as his finest accomplishment.

Aunt Hulda Banter, then living in Cleveland, was about to observe her eighty-eighth birthday anniversary and her only child, Mrs. Matthew Nute (our neighbor), was minded to telephone her congratulations. Mrs. Nute had finished churning and was wiping her hands prior to putting in the call. In those days the so-called Farmers' Line served the community and was connected in some remote way and remoter place with the Bell System. Everyone for miles around was on the same line, and it was always a task to get the Listening Toms to hang up, to reach the operator, and to convince her that an out-of-town call was not beyond the realm of possibility. Mrs. Nute had made up her mind.

She took down the receiver, stood on her tiptoes, and yelled into the wall-piece, "Git off'n the line, now, I'm going to call long distance!" Satisfied at the clicks she heard, she then cranked central and distinctly repeated her mother's number in Cleveland. The line buzzed and Mrs. Nute heard the operators relay the number. She mused on what she would say to her mother, and with half-closed eyes stared vacantly at the wallpaper and weighted this phrase against that.

Oscar, the Nute bull, had already torn down his stanchion, put the hired man up on the scafflings, tipped over the cart, and pulled up half the cabbages in the kitchen garden. While Mrs. Nute was patiently waiting her connection, Oscar was moving destructively toward the house. At this precise moment he bounded into the kitchen and shoved one foot through the cane bottom of the Boston rocker. This commotion and Oscar's immediate displeasure brought Mrs. Nute from her reverie and sent her headlong through the sitting room to round up a posse.

Oscar limped, rocker and all, to the telephone. He smelled at the dangling receiver and ran his tongue into the mouthpiece.

He did not know, of course, that the operators had skillfully performed their services, that Aunt Hulda was excitedly holding her 'phone to her ear, and that the Cleveland operator was intoning sweetly, "Here is your party. Go ahead, please!"

Oscar did not know that. But he might just as well. He laid back his ears, humped up his back, sucked in a torrent of wind, rolled his eyes, and blatted so the house shook. He then kicked the rocking chair into the pantry, knocked down the fernery, swished his tail into a pan of buttermilk, and went back to the kitchen garden where he was ultimately retrieved.

To this day, Aunt Hulda believes she was struck by lightning.

1944
A Pea Festival—for Sister Kate

W e've never exactly had a family reunion, although they are common in these parts and people have a good time. What we have had is a Pea Festival. Grandfather instituted these, and while they started out as a family gathering, they degenerated into a public outing and the congregation that gathered in our grove frequently included tourists who happened to be going by and got curious. After the old man had his gardens all in, he would sow two or three rows of green peas for the Festival, and allowing about 60 days for maturity he would send out the alarm.

Thus along late in August on an appointed Sunday the clan would gather, each division bringing neighbors and friends and everyone bringing something for everyone to eat. The gastronomic challenge was definitely insuperable, but we always did our best. The feast was built around a cauldron of green peas cooked over an open fire up under the oaks, and we always figured we had something unique in the way of picnics.

Upon arrival, each person was given a utensil of some sort and the rows of late peas were pointed out. Some had apple crates, some had milk pans, some had sap buckets, but everyone had something to pick in and the instructions were for everyone to pick and shell as many peas as he or she could eat. No two pickers estimated alike, and what usually happened was that every available pan, crock, box, bucket, and basket on the place was filled with peas. Youngsters filled strawberry baskets, oldsters patiently filled bushel measures. And then everyone sat around under the trees and shelled and shelled. Grandfather was the exception. He maintained that everyone had to share with him, and once a year he was going to have a mess of green peas that he neither picked, shelled, nor cooked. One of the old oak trees grew out over a shelving rock, making a most comfortable seat. Grandfather would sit there, leaning against the oak, and make regal remarks about his enviable situation. He called the seat his throne, and there he sat to be waited upon by old and young, a benevolent dictator who could eat his weight in peas.

Folks who came from the coast would bring clams and lobsters, and an uncle who had a store up country always brought yards and yards of thick beefsteak, a crate of oranges, and a pail of mulberry mixture. Every branch of the family brought its quota of pies and cakes. There was a special place between two big rocks for stacking watermelons. All in all, the appetites of the family were provided for, except that the peas always tasted so much better than anyone expected that much of the food went home again. A universal readership may not realize that a good Yankee meal can be made on green peas alone—if there are enough of them and they are well buttered, which there was and they were.

These Pea Festivals went along for a number of years, and

some folks would come several hundred miles to them. Then one year we had one under new management, and although the crowd was on hand as usual, the stone throne under the oak wasn't occupied all day and it didn't seem just exactly as before. We try to have a picnic up in the grove every year just the same, and we send out the usual alarm when the peas begin to pod. But lacking the attraction of Grandfather's unifying presence, the gathering is just a gathering, and we haven't called it either a reunion or a Pea Festival.

But we're having a Pea Festival this year, and you never saw such preparations as are going on. Word came that sister Kate, who has gone to war, is due home and her letter issued exact instructions as to how her spirits may be rejuvenated by the proper application of home-cooked provender. It seems that she has discovered a great truth once broadcast by Uncle Ralph, who wrote it in a book. He wrote a book on foreign cookery, and it contained two chapters. The first chapter said there isn't anything outside of New England fit for a Yankee to eat. The second chapter, concluding the treatise, said that if there were, nobody would know how to cook it. Sister Kate has therefore occupied her time away by reflecting greedily on the joys of an old-time Pea Festival, and she has ordered one intact.

To accommodate her furlough, we have peas all shelled and in the freezer. She is going to have a cream pie, corn on the cob, strawberry shortcake (also from the freezer), sugar-cured juniper-smoked fried ham, apple pan dowdy, buttermilk biscuits and honey, sour milk doughnuts, baked beans and brownbread, blueberry pie, Mother's yeast bread, haddock chowder, corned beef and cabbage, applesauce cake with chocolate frosting, and little things like that.

She asked for it; and we're going to make her sit on the throne and eat the whole business.

1944
Parthenogenesis—and Pat's Pats

Most beekeepers are extremely well informed about bees, and can tell the most amazing things. They talk for hours about the routine of the hive, and usually wind up by remarking casually that a drone bee has no father, but does have a maternal grandfather—". . . a clear case of parthenogenesis." I've always wondered where they found out, because I don't know much about bees. I always said they were made with stingers, and there wasn't much else to be said for them. But I'm certainly not an educated beekeeper.

We've always had bees, and I get along fine with them. We get honey, and they swarm now and then, and I let it go at that. I'm not an apiarist—I just keep them to pollenate the fruits and vegetables, and if I never got any honey I'd keep them just the same. But Pat Sawyer bought his bees for their honey.

When sugar tightened up, like many another, Pat bought a package of bees from down in Georgia, found a hive, and supposed he was going to raise his own sweets. But when the package came, it buzzed more than he had expected, and he hurried up here with them for instruction and assistance. This merely meant that I now had one more swarm of bees to take care of, and Pat's equity was rewarded by the privilege of lying on his stomach in the hot sun and watching the workers bring in pollen. At first he peeked around the barn, but in time he worked closer and closer until his nose rested on the landing board. He used to ask all sorts of questions I couldn't answer.

One day the bees swarmed, and I hived them and called Pat up. He was delighted to have two swarms for the price of one, and hurried up to inspect his augmentation. But when he got here the hive was empty—the bees had flown. He was courteous enough not to accuse me openly, but it was plain he felt some bungling of mine had cost him a swarm of bees. I was therefore glad to discover his bees in a hollow maple up in the woods. I had it half sawed down when the day warmed up and the buzzing attracted my attention. I called him on the telephone, and Pat hurried up with a washtub and a long-handled spoon to assist.

We sawed out the hollow part of the log and split it with wedges. As we scooped out the comb in two-foot-long sections, it occurred to me that Pat was talking most intelligently about bees. He had all the phrases and terms of an educated beekeeper, and he was taking great delight in telling me the answers to the questions he had asked last summer. He said a drone bee has no father, but does have a maternal grandfather, and I said, "A clear case of parthenogenesis." He gave me a funny look, and explained that he had been reading the ABC and XYZ of Bee Culture in his spare time. He said that apiculture depends wholly on an intimate knowledge of bees and their habits, and success comes only with precise information. "Bees are very friendly," he said, "and a man who understands them can do miracles with them."

It was precisely then that Pat took off his pants. We'd already had a few jabs on our hands, but long ago I began counting that part of the game. I always claim honey tastes better when you fight over it. So I naturally figured that Pat was merely demonstrating his proficiency at disrobing—for it appeared that his dexterity could come only from long practice. One moment he was clothed, and the next he wasn't, and I thought he was remarkably facile. Facility is also relative, however, for the first thing I knew I had mine off, too, and it was evident that my friend's agility had been bettered.

Our four legs now received a grooming, and he disposed of the bees that had crept up under his pants while I took care of mine. I never had them do that before (or behind, either), and it was something I'll watch out for in the future. I got four direct connections, and Pat said he got six bull's-eyes, and two others he wouldn't count. He said anything that went in less than six inches was superficial and a real beekeeper would ignore it. He said he was having so much fun nothing short of a musket ball would dissuade him.

We did have a good time, at that, and we brought the honey up to the house for everyone to see, and the women wanted to know if we'd got stung. "No," said Pat, "nothing to speak of. Bees are very friendly if you know how to handle them."

"Tell them about the parthenogenesis," I said.

Pat's wife said, "I'd rather hear about how you two happen to have each other's pants on."

1945
Fourth-of-July Shortcake at Gramp's

We had a nice Fourth of July this year. We didn't have any green peas, because the way this season is going we'll be lucky if we have any by Thanksgiving, and we didn't have any salmon because I didn't get to catch one. But we had some strawberries, and when I can have strawberries for the Fourth of July, I don't care if school keeps or not. And the reason may be a story of sorts.

It goes back to the time I was in short pants—which isn't too definite a time, because in my day we wore short pants right into high school, and a fellow was usually shaving before he got long ones. But there I was, and along came Aunt Lillian. She worked in an office (still does, for that matter) and she had a long week end for the Fourth. So she thought she'd come up here to the old farm to visit her father, who was my grandfather, and she came and got me to go with her. I hadn't got acquainted with the old gentleman at that time, and was really a village kid; so the jaunt impressed me from beginning to end—particularly the long ride on a trolley car out through the country. Trolley cars to me went in subways or along streets. This one went right through the woods lickety-split, and pretty soon we were at the Falls.

Aunt Lillian hadn't told Grampie we were coming; so we went across the street to the hotel, and went right into the livery stable where men were sitting back on benches and complaining that firecrackers scairt the hosses. Aunt Lillian called for a conveyance, and while one man threw the harness on a black mare, another took the fills and backed out a surrey, and away we went with the man up front telling us we might get a good ride if some tarnation boy hove a firecracker at the right time.

It was cool when we left my home early that Fourth, and it was cool riding on the trolley with the windows open. But the day had advanced, and the sun had climbed—and we could have popped corn right on the seat of that surrey. I remember how the leaves on the trees hung limp along the road, and how the dust rose up and choked us, and how the horse hardly got out of her own way going up Hinckley's Hill. The road is paved now, and the hill isn't so steep.

All this took time, and the day was hot, and I was a youngster, and I thought we'd never get to the old farm house. And when we did arrive, and my Aunt paid 50 cents for the ride of two and a half miles, Grampie wasn't home.

"Oh, dear," she said, "I should have written we were coming."

"He can't be far," I said. "The door isn't locked," not understanding that the old doors had no locks, and the house was shut up only in the winter to keep out the cold.

The buggy was in the shed. And the horses were harnessed and out.

"He's working in the fields," Aunt Lillian said, and we found him away up on the hogback piece cultivating tomatoes—the horse half asleep and navigating from memory, Grandfather wringing wet in the sun, and the reins around his neck so if the horse ever had run away it would have taught him a lesson.

"Oh, Lil," he said, and he is the only person I ever heard call her anything shorter than Lillian, "I'm so glad you've come. I was just wishing for an excuse to stop work."

At that time, of course, I had a silly notion the Fourth of July was excuse enough for anybody, but since he didn't think so, and since the day was so very hot, I'm sure he really was glad to see us. He unhitched and left the cultivator right in the row, tied the reins to the bridle, and the horse followed us back toward the house.

Half-way back, we stopped and picked strawberries. These were tame ones—Gramp raised them by the cartload and was supposed to have a secret. We picked his hat full, and Aunt Lillian's hat full, and my hat full, and then we cupped our hands against our chests and piled them up.

Aunt Lillian made a shortcake. It was about a rod long and two hoe-handles wide, and as thick as that, and we had berries enough to frighten a wholesaler, and it was the first time I ever knew Aunt Lillian could cook. None of your sweetcake: this was the real stuff! Short as a flicker, and browned to the neatest crunch of a crust. We didn't bother with whipped cream, it being well known that prudent folks add nothing to distort the fundamental excellence. That's all we had to eat, and we ate every acre of it, and Grandfather drove us back to the Falls in the evening, and I grew up to have a certain extra meaning for the Fourth of July. I always cultivate the tomatoes, and eat a shortcake.

I'll probably get tossed out of the house when this is printed—

but do you want to know something? Nobody ever made as good a strawberry shortcake as that one of Aunt Lillian's. I know, because Grampie said so.

1945
A Christmas Day's Wages

All of 60 years ago, a deaf-mute lived in the house on the curve just this side of Purinton's Corner, a man who lived alone and took it for granted that nobody would say anything to him or expect him to answer, because everybody knew him. His name was Billie Dunn, he asked no favors, and a wave of the hand was all he ever got or gave as he took his abbreviated place in the goings-on of the community.

Billie used to come up here to the farm now and then. He would arrive about 6 o'clock on a bitter cold morning, the frost formed in his beard, and his copper-toed boots frozen solid from the long hike up the road. Nobody knew he was coming; he simply walked into the old kitchen, stomped his feet by the door and swept off with the broom left handy for that purpose. No matter who you were, in those winter days you knew that you were expected to reach in through the door and feel for the broom handle that would be there, then sweep your feet. Billie would sweep his feet in his own silence, but nobody in the kitchen said anything. Grandfather and Grandmother and all the aunts and uncles were having breakfast and when they saw it was Billie Dunn they kept right on having breakfast.

Had it been anyone else, there'd have been a welcome; at least Mary would have pushed Eddie and Helen to one side and set an extra place while Grandmother dished up another bowl of porridge. But Billie was no stranger, and Billie had his own way of doing business. There was, suiting the need, a wave of the hand between him and Grandfather, but that was all.

Then Billie would begin taking off his clothes, down to the homespun breeches and the thick woolen shirt, and he'd hang them behind the door as if this were his own home and he had rules about being neat. Next he would warm his hands at the fire, and then he would go to the cupboard and get himself a bowl and a plate. He'd bring in some eggs, slice off a piece of ham, and locate whatever else lay around useful for breakfast. He'd break the eggs in the spider, turn them neatly, let his ham get just right, and after taking up a bowl of oatmeal he'd come over to the table and sit down.

After a hearty breakfast, he'd stack his dishes by the sink, put on his heavy clothes again, go out to the woodshed, take down the bucksaw—and until noon he'd buck wood steadily and tirelessly while the world went ahead more or less without him. He usually stopped precisely on the dot of dinner time, but sometimes one of the children would have to go out and tug at his sleeve and stick a thumb in the mouth to convey the idea. After dinner he bucked wood again until supper, and after supper he stacked his dishes again and then went over to the corner table where Grandmother kept her butter and egg accounts. He'd find a piece of paper, scratch on it the price of his day's work— 25¢. Grandfather would give Billie 25¢, and Billie would walk the four miles home again and it would sometimes be a month or more before the folks here saw him again.

Billie was not actually under standard mentally. Grandfather always felt he liked to participate in the home life that went on here, and made sawing wood his excuse for sitting down three times to a generous meal amongst others. The 25¢ was nothing but a token payment, and was not intended to represent the value of labor exerted. At least, 25¢ was far less than the going price even in those mellow days.

But Billie came one morning which happened to be Christmas. The children were in festive mood, and Grandmother had a big holiday dinner to prepare. Grandfather and the boys had intended to sit around most of the time. Knowing Billie, nobody tried an explanation, so he went ahead and sawed wood all day, and had a slam-bang dinner with bag pudding and everything else, and if he wasn't aware of the date he certainly betrayed no astonishment at the fare.

Grandfather waited until Billie had written down his "25¢," and then he gave him a dollar, on account of its being Christmas, and Billie seemed pleased and went home. Grandmother thought it was very nice to be able to cheer the old fellow up with some extra cooking, and Grandfather felt infinitely philanthropic and counted the extra well worth doing.

Some stories point their own morals, and sometimes the moral has to be dragged in by the ears, and sometimes there doesn't seem to be any. Maybe there isn't any here, after all, but I always liked the story a great deal, because the next day Billie Dunn hiked all the way back to the farm and brought 75¢ change.

1946
Governor Lays Cornerstone at Gould Farm

I n a surprise move, Gov. Horace A. Hildreth of Maine today laid the cornerstone of the new house which John Gould, author and farmer, is building on the Ridge.

Learning about the work while on one of his whirlwind campaign tours around the Pine Tree State, Governor Hildreth visited the farm, finding there, as he said, "more people than down to the Falls."

He was just in time for the cornerstone laying, and placed an Army ammunition box inside the stone, plastering it down heavily with cement.

The box contained, among other things, a copy of Mr. Gould's book, "Farmer Takes a Wife," a copy of the current week's issue of the *Lisbon Enterprise*, which Mr. Gould publishes; a copy of the Aug. 22 issue of the *Christian Science Monitor* with its "Dispatch from the Farm"; a picture of the Gould family, including Mr. and Mrs. Gould, "Little John," and "Kathie," and a letter with the names of all the workmen on the job.

Also included in the contents of the box was an ear of seed corn from the Gould farm.

Governor Hildreth removed a "Hildreth-for-Governor" campaign button from his own coat, and added that to the collection.

On top of the cornerstone was placed a slab of marble salvaged from the old First National Bank Building of Boston at the time it was razed, and which, according to Mr. Gould, "has been kicking around the farm" for a long time.

The brief ceremonies over, Governor Hildreth munched on an apple from the farm orchard, and partook of other refreshments served.

Footnote: Another Dispatch from the Farm,"Be-Kind-to-Hornets Week Celebrated" appears on the Editorial Page today.

Another footnote: In those days the *Monitor* published a Boston city edition. Everett M. Smith, assistant city editor, took this story over the telephone from Governor Hildreth's campaign manager, who ate three pieces of gravenstein apple pie.

1946
Be-Kind-to-Hornets Week
Celebrated

It seems as if somewhere is a lovely story about holding up construction because the carpenters wouldn't disturb a mother robin who was hatching her little ones on the scaffolding. This can be justified, even if it cost a pretty penny. Naturally, anyone with the right streak of rainbow through his gristle, coming to the building of a house, would like some such lovely yarn worked into his joists and planking.

It's probably just that we live in Maine. Maine is like that. We have robins, and they build nests, and the years come and go and about all the story we get is to tell bug-eyed tourists that our angleworms are so big they pull robins right into the ground. So no robin, or bluebird, came to incubate on our vestibule or crossmembers.

What we did get was a nest of hornets. I was a trifle disappointed, and thought it would be difficult, later, to regale our guests with the story so it would sound at all as charming as the one about the robin. Hardly anyone is glad to find a hornets' nest, and the discovery is seldom heralded as a boon. Dickie Janosco found this one. He was dismantling a pile of new boards, and was feeding them through the planer so everybody could get to boarding-in. Dickie didn't jump more than eight or ten feet, and as the altitude imparted an oracular tone to his remarks, everybody in miles was tuned in and informed.

Interest mounted, and the carpenters retired a short distance and conferred. They decided hornets' nests are a problem of the contractee, who is me, and that work would now be suspended while I thought of some way to render the situation more amenable. It is just barely possible that at this time I remembered the story of the robin.

The carpenters and Dickie were not unsympathetic. They cupped their hands over their mouths and offered advice. They suggested I would be cruel to interrupt this ordered arrangement of nature. They said the poor hornets had merely moved in to join in the great industry now evident. They said the hornets had every right to the boards I had, and that they, for one (they said), would stand firm on that principle. They indicated in general that nobody expected me to be able to do much about it.

The solution was really simple. I went near enough to get stung once, and after backing up several yards I turned around and went to the barn for my bee veil and mittens. The hornets bumped against this screening and backed up to bump again, but it didn't do much good. I shoved a plug into the little hole in the bottom of the nest, and except for a few loose hornets who flew around and around and let on they were mad at me, everything was under control.

It then came to mind that possibly the carpenters would like to see at close range just how I had solved this distressing problem, and I picked up the pine board with the nest attached and walked toward them with reassuring tone and valuable instruction. I pointed out that frequently our most trying difficulties can be instantly erased by no more effort than it took to plug a hornets' nest. I said if they would but look, this basic philosophic truth would be immediately apparent, and they would forever after thank me gratefully for both the information and the example.

But probably we shall always have with us the incapable, and these men refused absolutely to partake of the clear, cool water from my fountain of knowledge. They climbed up on the ladders, and went under the corn crib, and thus eluded their opportunity.

Then I carried the hornets out in the field, and uncorked them, and returned to find that the situation around our construction job had eased. Dick was back at his boards, and hammers were going, and nobody had very much to say about hornets. It may have been earlier, but certainly at that moment the robin came to mind, and I was pleased again about this business of living in Maine. I wouldn't have had anywhere near so much fun with a robin.

1947
Making the Most of a Lad Underfoot

They didn't have any school today for the bus children, the hills being icy, so the lad stayed home with me and worked the day as a carpenter. It cleared off and melted right away, but the school department couldn't help it, so we had a nice day at the expense of a few old arithmetic problems and such.

But school isn't the only place to learn. The lad's teacher is good at arithmetic problems and such, but she doesn't know much about carpentry. The house is swarming with carpenters, and we are now in the finishing-off stage. Every kind of tool is lying around to be tried, and much headway was made in the art of woodworking, so I doubt if the day was lost to the cause of education.

Not many houses are built the way we are building this one. Our intended living-room is filled with power tools, and every man has his chest and handbox on the job, so we are equipped for many an old-fashioned task that nowadays is largely taken care of in the lumber mills. We are tonguing and grooving our own pine panels, for one thing, and have the tools to do it. This makes more shavings than most modern houses accumulate a-building, and shavings definitely have an appeal to the children.

Sight of a carpenter slowly walking back and forth the length of a wide pine board to cut the beading along the edge naturally leads a lad to wonder if he can do it, so when the carpenter has laid his tool down to go out and get another board, the lad naturally picks it up and wanders up into the west bedroom to find out. I wouldn't think so much of the youngster if he didn't, and the carpenters on our job don't mind. Today, everybody did about half a day's work. The rest of the time they were explaining, demonstrating, or retrieving tools.

One fellow was ripping out some drip strips to go over the garage doors, which calls for sawing on an angle, and the lad stepped over to help pull the strips away from the saw table. In so doing he pinched the kerf together and this bound the saw. When the saw binds the motor runs hot. When the motor gets too hot it shuts itself off and has to cool.

So the carpenter coached the lad while the motor was cooling, and we learned that the kerf should be spread instead of pinched, that the strips should be drawn off in a straight line and never twisted, and that nobody ever reaches his hand over the edge of the table. By that time the motor was cool, the saw was going again, and after that the lad came running whenever anybody started up a power tool.

A smart carpenter keeps the boy underfoot working for him, and doesn't fight back. If you know anything, you don't say, "Stand aside now, Sonny, you're in the way." Instead, you say, "I wonder would you help me here a minute?" The lad leaps to assist, and you allow him to hold the other end of a board. The other end of the board doesn't need holding, and is probably already nailed in place, but the lad holds it until he is exhausted and his eyes bug out, and he comes away with a gratifying sense of having done a lot of heavy work.

So the lad got his share of boards to hold, horses to steady, and for an hour or so he was upstairs dangling a string down a hole to help the plumber. The plumber thought this up and then went home early and forgot to mention it, so I rolled up the string after a time and asked the lad why he didn't stand by the bench and make something.

So he made a chair for Teena's doll. Teena is the little girl next house up the road and she has a new birthday doll and nothing to set it in. In manufacturing this chair, which was really well done, every carpenter on the job donated his tools, and several of them even helped. The legs were tongued and grooved, and the seat had mortising. The best construction practices were used throughout.

I made him plane every piece, so he'd find out how to plane, and then he sandpapered all the sand off a sheet of sandpaper and nailed the thing together. One of the carpenters showed him where he'd planed the wrong way and left marks. "You should've turned the stick end for end." So we explained about the grain in wood, and how to find out which end of a board to work from.

At supper he explained this grain business to his mother, who was pleased, and told his sister all about the chair. His sister was not pleased, and indicated sisters have just as much use for dolls' chairs as little girls one house up the road.

But he took care of that neatly. "Next time there's no school I'll make you one, and it'll be a better one because I'm learning all the time."

1947
It Takes a Heap o'
Baking . . .

Acatastrophe of immeasurable proportions struck our happy home Saturday evening at precisely 5:45 o'clock, at which time our lady was removing the pot of beans from the oven, and the bottom dropped out of it. I can't stress too much the horror of the moment. I know of nothing in the history of mankind comparable to it.

We had fried eggs and bacon instead. We aren't sure just what happened. We think there was a fault in the pot, and as Saturday succeeded Saturday the constant addition of patina, essence, sheen and glory got to be too much for it, and the fault gave way and the bottom dropped out.

There was our baking of beans on the floor, swimming around gamely in their own juice, the shards sticking up around them like landmarks in the breakers, and my wife holding the handle of the pot in a holder and looking most helpless and forlorn. The handle was still attached to the neck and shoulders of the pot, but the pot was no longer a thing of beauty and a joy forever.

She said, faintly and with extreme evenness of tone, "The bottom fell out of the bean pot." It was even so. There had been a snap just as the pot cleared the floor of the oven, then a kind of swishing noise, and a splattering mushing. The pussycat came leaping toward the scene with investigative enthusiasm and a swirl of steam enveloped her, at which she backed up ten feet and looked unhappy.

I scooped the beans up into a pail, dipped up the juice with a ladle, mopped up all around the stove, and took our nice Saturday night beans down to the hens. When I came back the spider was on the stove, bacon was in the air, and she was cracking eggs.

Naturally it didn't seem like Saturday night at all. Naturally a spirit of disappointment prevailed. Friday night she had picked over three cups of dried beans, put them to soak, and all day she had been tending them. She kept the fire going for them; she added water when needed. She took the cover off at half-past three and browned the top with its bonnet of salt pork. And by half-past five they were ready.

She blew the horn as usual, and we came in to wash up and comment dutifully on the fine aroma that prevailed—not only in and about the house, but for some distance around outside. We made guesses as to what strange and delectable dish could be awaiting us this fine Saturday night, and we guessed roast beef, pork pie, lamb stew, and even broiled halves of milk-fed spring duckling. Then we guessed beans, and meant it.

But the catastrophe I speak of wasn't just the loss of the beans. That was a disappointment only, an unfortunate accident that merely changed our plans. The catastrophe involved the pot itself. You just don't bake beans in any old thing and it takes years and years to work a new crockery bean pot up into something that will bake a decent bean. Anybody knows that.

We'd had this bean pot ever since we went to housekeeping. It was given us by an understanding aunt of the old school who said, "By the time you have a family to enjoy it, it'll be fit to bake a bean in." She knew what she was talking about. The pores of a bean pot take on a mellowing, and it comes only from weekly bakings over a long, long time.

It takes barrels of beans, gallons of molasses, whole saltings of pork, bushels of onions, and months of blue moons to fire the quintessence into a good bean pot. The hand of the potter lacks the master touch. It takes the loving care of a mother to pick and choose only the right beans, and the right kinds of beans. It takes hot hardwood fires, and other things in the oven at the same time—punkin pies, sheets of caraway cookies, johnny cake, and all such as that. It takes years, and none but the old, established families really get the best baked beans.

So the catastrophe struck, and the bean pot is a total loss. During this week we'll pick up a new pot at the store, and it will be shiny and clean and not worth a cent. Beans next Saturday will be just like anybody's beans. It will be away along next fall before we can expect the new bean pot to start getting into shape. I hope it isn't too long a summer.

1948
Tricks of Sapping—and March Snow

An element of perturbation accompanies the sight of one's only daughter sinking out of sight in a snowbank, even if you know she won't go far and will be back soon. When she happens to be five and has trudged up into the maple orchard for her first drip from the first spile, and has been trustful beyond completeness in a strange place, and then disappears in a snowbank, the most perturbing part is your realization that *she* thinks *you* did it on purpose.

That's the way of it. I wasn't going to bring up, here, sapping this spring, thinking a new topic would do better. But sapping turns out to be always new, and this year it was wholly new for Kathie. Five-year legs are pretty short for March snow.

March brings us this corn snow, and the cold nights freeze a crust on it. I can walk on the crust until some time in the forenoon, and then the sun begins to work. For a time I can walk on some of it, but not all of it—depending on light and shadow. So snowshoes are a good rig the first few days of sapping, and then you have the paths beaten down and can walk anywhere.

Kathie couldn't use snow shoes, but she could walk on top of the crust long after it refused to support my weight even in the shadows. There was something fairylike about the way she skipped along, and something a little too adult in her joy as she watched me flounder and fall through, snowshoes and all.

This time of year when the snow settles under your snow-shoes, it doesn't just settle under one foot at a time. It collapses for 10 feet 'round about. You might get the same sensation if you were standing in your kitchen quietly frying smelts and the whole floor suddenly went through into the cellar. The act of stopping is just as astounding, at the time, as the act of falling. When sapping, you have buckets under your arm, and maybe an ax, and a few things that add to the sensation and also to the noise and hilarity among children.

Besides, you never know just which step is going to take you on down, and which will stay up, and you walk along expecting to both stay up and go down, but never quite being sure. Kathie experienced none of this, but darted around amongst the trees and had a fine time, and stopped now and then to laugh at Daddy floundering.

Well, we went through the springtime ritual the way all dis-cerning parents should instruct their young. There were some words about the vernal rejuvenation of nature, the cycle of vege-tation, the principle of capillary attraction, and the excellence of carbohydrates as plant food. She got more of it than I expected, because she repeated it to her mother later; and her mother said, "You, and the way you talk to those poor kids!"

I was unable to get "spile" across as a word. To Kathie, it is a "spike"—and I drove in the first spike and showed her how to loop her tongue around the end to get the first milky exudation of wonder and delight. She found it was sweet, and she was initiated into a fraternity whose annual meetings I hope she never grows too old to attend.

This was fine, and she derived extra-special joy from the fact that Brother, who is already an old hand at sapping, was in school and couldn't attend. This trek with Daddy was all hers, and there was to be dinner by the spring, even, and everything was fine and dandy.

Now two big pines stand where the land drops off to the brook, and any winter will lay 15 feet of snow in there, as if the land didn't slope off at all. This winter had done a little better. As the warming sun returns to us, and the brook underneath this drift stirs to life, nature removes a good part of the catch, and leaves the hard-driven top just as it was. It is a mantrap, and I've learned to go around. I supposed Kathie's nimble weight would be supported all right, and I looked up to see her coming between the pines jubilant and trusting. Then she simply disappeared.

The rescue took but a moment. The only harm done was to ruin her complete faith in Father as a tutor in the wilds. She indicated a belief that this had all been planned, and the same thing as set up solely to catch her.

She felt this was one of the regular things that are planned for the eager child out to learn the tricks of sapping. This was one of the tricks, and very dirty. The bottom drops out of everything, and you find yourself alone in a hole. She wouldn't get off her hands and knees the rest of the day, and I don't think she gave full credence to anything I said afterward.

There was this feeling that Kathie thought I was pretty grand, being nice to her on a very special occasion, and then I had to reach down and grab her by the collar, and I found her ardor had been dampened, her devotion dimmed, and her trust clouded with doubt.

1948
A Day for Fathers and Sons

O ne trouble with me is I don't always recognize an opportunity. Mother was more observant. "Don't you have a nice daddy?" she said. The lad said he guessed so, whereat Kathie hurried to say that she did, too, and as a result I found I had neglected to recognize a day-long opportunity of magnificent proportions.

In the beginning I had a purpose. I was to make up to the lad on Saturdays for the deficiencies of our modern school system—which I say without my tongue in anybody's cheek and mean it. I don't wish to stir up a hullabaloo, but it seemed to me the public program of intellectual instigation is deficient in a good many of the ethics, and in most of the practical applications. And for a boy out in the country it is fatiguing. He rides on a bus and puts in more hours a day than you do—whatever you do.

So Saturday was to be my day to get off alone with him and balance the accounts, sort of, and see that his values were secure, and overcome any false starts, if any. We have done that now for quite a spell, and Saturday is the best day in the week.

So we laid plans to build a new maple sap house up in the woods, and Friday night we loaded the trailer with lumber and tools so we could get an early start, and last Saturday we struck out right after breakfast.

The woods, this fall, have been a riot of indescribable beauty. Anybody with a maple sugar bush has had more wealth than he deserves, and it was in this profusion of loveliness that we went to work. We cleared out some small growth and set our corner posts. We fashioned the four-by-eight main timbers. It's to be a small camp, just big enough for our size evaporator, and nothing fancy. We're using scrap timber, and if the lad saws crooked it does no great harm. He has to learn to saw straight some time, and here's good practice.

We talked of this and that, the way we do of a Saturday. I showed him how to mark a board on two sides for sawing. He doesn't have too good an "eye," as we say, and he needs guide lines. The camp came along fast. We got the floor timbers in, and boarded over, and had studs up for one side when our stomachs told us it was noon. Nothing but an apple apiece and plenty of cold spring water to make our teeth snap all morning, and small wonder our stomachs were running fast.

It was only 11:30, really, and while we thought about going to the house for dinner we heard a shout up the woodroad, and there came Mother and Kathie with the picnic things. We had a fire going in no time, and boards laid out for a table.

The ham sizzled and spit and I wondered why people for miles around didn't come to get some—the noise it made. The lad said he could eat three eggs, but Mother moderately modified that to two, and later was proved correct. It had been baking morning back at the house, so we had new bread, and some still-hot doughnuts, and we made out.

Mother and Kathie wet down the fire and packed up the dirty dishes and started for the house. The lad and I were back sawing and hammering again, and we had a fine afternoon, too. It cooled off quickly in the evening, so we knocked off to be home before dark. It seemed as if our noon dinner hadn't stayed with us, because supper tasted as if we hadn't eaten in weeks.

Then, after supper, Mother said, "I hope you realize what a nice daddy you've got," and the lad said he guessed he did. Mother said, "You remember what happened to those boys in the village?"

"What boys?"

"The ones who stole some lumber, and swiped Mr. Harrison's nails, and cut down all the trees, and made a camp."

"Oh, them—yes."

"Well, that's because they didn't have a daddy to show them how to do things right, and they got off on the wrong foot, and got into trouble."

"They've all got daddies," the lad said.

"Yes, everybody has a daddy—that's what makes the difference, and I hope you understand it and appreciate it."

Well, of course, I felt like the shiny side of a million dollars, but I was a little put out that I had missed this comparison myself. The truth is, I have so much fun on these Saturdays, I just neglect to embrace the question, and all I think about is what a promising son I have. I know I shouldn't mention it this way, with such unbecoming frankness, but even if both of us miss the point, we'll still have a new sap house come spring.

1949
Chicken-Fat Fraternity

Being an old pie-maker of some ability, I was naturally interested in the contest recently conducted in Massachusetts to see who could make the best pie. The contestants were limited somewhat by rules that said the filling had to be Massachusetts cranberries and Massachusetts apples together, which I think was too bad. I think there are better fillings, myself, but I don't wish to start a fight over this, and I will go on to other considerations:

Last summer, my family took a whim that they would like to

go to the seashore, so they went down to the seashore. I went down evenings before supper and came back up mornings after breakfast, and managed to make out. I discovered one day that the Red Astrachans had come of age, and lacking any loving hands about to bake me a pie, I baked one myself.

It is not hard to bake a pie and it is just as easy to bake a good pie. So I baked this one, and it was a dandy. Just as it was due to be brought from the oven, there came a knock at the back door. Hastily throwing off my ap'n, I opened the door and there stood a group of tourists.

I imply no particular connotative extra by calling them tourists. They were touring. They had two automobiles and were together. I think they were from Illinois, but it may have been Michigan. All southern states are alike from up here. It might have been Dakota. Anyway, they said they read these Dispatches, which is always pleasant to hear, and they were passing through Maine and had been looking forward to viewing the locale of so many whoppers. They seemed very fine folks, ranging from Grandmother down to a sprout in a playsuit, and I had been introduced about halfway around when a thought came into my head, and I said:

"Oh! Wait'll I take my pie out!"

They didn't believe a bit of what they saw, but they watched through the screen door while I extracted my masterpiece. It was a golden brown, just right, and it steamed good, so the savor went to the far corners of the farm and put on an advertising campaign. When I came back to the door these people had their faces given over to a downright air of incredulity and amazement, with a touch of profound admiration. Somebody asked, "D-do you bake pies?"

"Oh, yes," I said, throwing the thing off as if it were nothing—you should see my tatting and needlepoint. If I had arranged the whole thing for theatrical effect, it couldn't have been better. "Oh, yes," I said, as if I baked pies all day long for months at a time. Actually, it was the first pie I had baked in weeks. But it was good, and I carried it to the seashore that evening with a little jar of cream to pour over it, and everybody said it was good. So, you see, I know something about pies.

Well, after this woman won the Massachusetts pie contest—her name is Kay Mitchell and she lives at Wrentham—a grocery store outfit made a big thing out of the fact that she used their flour. They went on the radio and everything, and said she used their flour, and pointed out it was no wonder she won. They suggested anybody who could tote home a bag of this flour would immediately be a pie champeen. They are full of prunes, because in the *New England Homestead* they have just printed Mrs. Mitchell's recipe, and the real secret is out. I find she is a member of my own happy fraternity, and, like me, she knows, she knows.

Chicken fat!

Her pastry mix includes one teaspoon of chicken fat. It isn't much, but it's the difference between anybody's pie and that of a winner. Mrs. Mitchell might well have been looking over my shoulder that day the tourists came. If you use chicken fat you can make a prize-winning pie out of any old flour. If you use chicken fat you can even make a pie out of Massachusetts cranberries and Massachus—but I wasn't going to say that. First, though, you have to have chicken fat.

Back during the war when the government knew more about farming than anybody and it was hard to buy grain, I grew a good bit of yellow corn. At one time my hens lived on it exclusively. It made the eggs very yellow and made the hens very fat. Whenever we stewed one for Sunday dinner, which was then about every Sunday, we would end up with another pail of chicken fat. We used it for everything. It was magic. We never ate better before or since. A little daub of it in the batter at the right time will cheer up everybody around.

Chicken fat! Remember that. And while Mrs. Mitchell is currently being memorialized because she uses somebody's special blend of bleached, rarefied, emulsicated, fortituted, splenderized and scarifacted flour, don't be misled. If you want a good pie, never mind whose flour you use—just put in some chicken fat.

1949
Popcorn on the Indian Trail

I t says here in this magazine that an Indian named Quade-quina brought a bushel of popped popcorn to the Pilgrims for Thanksgiving in 1630, and that popcorn is now a major American industry. This is good. But the story doesn't tell me how Quadequina popped the stuff, and it is an item of information I've wondered about for a long time. It would be entertaining and instructive to consider the important feature of popcorn at Thanksgiving feasts, but more enticing to me is a consideration of how the Indians fabricated the confection in the primitive wilds.

One evening long ago, Grandfather and I were munching popcorn in the old farmhouse, and he said the Indians used to take popcorn on the trail. No need to weight yourself down with heavy provender. Travel light and eat hearty. A handful of popcorn would make several meals. I lifted my youthful face, aglow with the thirst for knowledge, and asked Grampie how the Indians popped it.

Grampie looked at me, indicating he hadn't ever thought of that, and suggested it was bedtime. Always after that, whenever he was yanking the big sheet-metal popper back and forth over the red-hot top of the Queen Atlantic, he would wag his head. He never figured it out. It is a moot question.

The simple children of the forest must have had some method

of converting the kernels into full-fashioned fare. There were no tin-plate or woven-wire utensils in the dim beginnings of North American popcorn culture, and if the Indian had something else to tame his jumping maize, it would make an interesting piece of news—particularly if it was a device he could use miles from the tepee on a business trip.

I have pictured the agile brave leaping about in a rod circumference around a redhot rock, chasing down his popping corn before Adjidaumo beat him to it. Such activity would take fat off quicker than corn would put it on, and the legends in our family never told of a brave that agile or that active. A long, tiring day on the trail would make going hungry rather attractive if that had to be the way to get supper.

I have never had any luck picturing the Indian with a corn popper. I can't seem to imagine him treading along the forest path, his moccasins lightly touching the moss, a bunnyskin of popcorn swinging at his belt, his bow and arrow at the ready, and a popcorn popper under his nether arm.

There is no record I know of in which an Indian, confused in the excitement of a massacre, forgets which hand his tomahawk is in, and bops a surprised pioneer behind the ear with a long-handled popcorn popper. That would have happened, surely, because at Potts's Point in 1654 an Indian who was surprised by a volley of musketry from the Holbrook henhouse tossed away his paddle and began making his canoe go with a flitch of bacon—a natural reversal in such circumstances.

So I don't believe the Indians had popcorn poppers, or we'd have known about it long ago.

The spider, as frying pans have been called in New England since Priscilla first fried clams for John, was no doubt the Pilgrim's contribution to the popcorn industry. A kivver on a spider does first rate. The Indians had no such device. In fact, cooking was more or less haphazard with them. Some things they hung in smoke; others they buried in coals.

They knew how to heat a rock and roast lobsters. They could

heat small round stones and drop them in water—which is the way they are supposed to have boiled down maple sap. I don't believe it myself, as that would have taken too many rocks and too long a time, and the Indians were not essentially perseverant in most things. They knew how to roll ducks and fish in blue clay and roast them, but, of course, doing that with a handful of popcorn would have resulted in an explosion that would have had the Russians competing furiously even in that day.

I suppose the hot, flat rock is the best bet, but I don't feel like accepting it as proved. Suppose we get a rock hot, and toss on a handful of popping kernels. See the result! The air is full of flying white popcorn, and all we have to do now is hunt through the junipers, sweetfern, hardhack, alders, hackmatack and blueberry bushes and find enough to satisfy a hungry Indian. This will take us a long time, and now we are even more hungry; the rock has cooled off, night is coming on, and we can see it is no fun to pop corn in the uncharted wilderness.

If Quadequina had a bushel of popcorn for Thanksgiving at Plymouth, he must have been popping it since April. All we know is that he had it, and delivered it, and in 1630 the popcorn industry was founded. I'd still like to know how he popped it.

[Editor's Note—Reluctant as we are to admit it, we share John's popcorn perplexity, and it apparently is shared in OTHER founts of knowledge even in some important cities of learning. But we have humbly found that where the more obvious sources fail, one or more of our readers is sure to pop up with the right answer. We'll be waiting on the trail.]

1950
Maple Sirup and Memories

Quand vous serez bien vieille . . ."

Those were my very words, although I had to come back to the house and look in the book to see what they were in French. I was speaking to my daughter Kathryn, and the locale for the colloquy was our sugarhouse with steam rolling out the ventilators.

Every year at this time I fight off the idea of doing another piece about maple sirup. It's an old story, and has been written up a lot of times even by people who don't know much about it. It is, nonetheless, an inexhaustible topic, because something new always happens to give you a fresh approach. It is also a popular topic, because maple sweets are about as good as you'll find, and most people never seem to tire of the topic or the product. So this year I found myself saying, "When you're an old lady . . ."

To Kathie, that prospect is infinitely remote, of course, and at seven short years her ideas about memories wouldn't seem to be advanced. But it was memories I was talking about. All over the world are elderly people, some of them not so old, either, who stir uneasily in their places this time of year and think fondly of numerous things in their childhoods.

Those who have sugar places in their memories have something overwonderful, and it's a fine thing to know that once again the March winds are flailing the tops of the maples, and if you could be there once again you could hear the drip in the bucket—you could hear the whole symphony of many drips in many buckets, all different tones and distances. Snow fleas lining the deep footprints in the snow, a spring crow gliding in with a squawk after his long pull up from Carolina, the yelp of a bluejay who wishes he'd stayed away, and the chatter of chickadees pecking at the suet you've brought along to nail up over the sugarhouse door. It's a great thing.

Well, Kathie got off the school bus. I knew it was time because the dog took a sneak. The dog knows when the bus is due, and he goes back to the house to be on hand and make sure everybody knows he's still on duty. (The lad is on the bus, too, but I'm counting him out of this discussion because he's an old hand at sapping, and had his time at the rudiments some years back.)

It's quite a hike from the house up, and Kathie has to have her lunch before she starts up. That's probably what the dog has in mind, as much as anything, because the first I see of Kathie, she's trudging down the wood road holding her last cookie aloft with the dog jumping at it hopefully, and Kathie's remonstrative remarks ringing through the forest.

I find a greeting on such an occasion has to follow certain amenities. To begin with, I am supposed to be too surprised to speak. Whoever suspected seeing her there?

"I walked up!" she said. This appeared to have some foundation in fact, and I expressed an opinion that it was a good job, well done.

"Making sap?" she called.

"I'm making something better than sap."

"It's smoking," she said.

"That's steam."

"It looks like smoke."

"All right, it's smoke, then. Come in here."

With the tin dipper I got her a drink of sap from the tank, cold, with that trace of maple sweetness so highly prized. Aqua pura has been widely advertised as an excellent beverage, but sap has a springtime advantage. With a bountiful bubbling spring right by the saphouse we don't touch the water as long as the maples run. Water never boiled an egg so it tastes like one that has been left three minutes and a half in the evaporator—ask anybody who has ever had such an egg. So Kathie had her taste of sap, and she paused between the first and second long pull to say, "Good!"

Then I held the dipper under the spigot on the sirup tank, and drew off some of the hot liquid. It wasn't within six degrees of sirup, yet, but it was concentrated considerably beyond the sap stage. Scalding hot, it had to be cooled, so I set the dipper on the snow. I'm not talking about sugar on snow—that's a different matter. This was merely half-cooked sirup from the far end of the pan—still watery, but amber and deliciously sweet.

When it was cooled down to mere warmness, she sat on the steps of the sugarhouse and tried it. The look of anticipation was nothing compared to her look of realization. I doubt if anybody, in all the history of the world, ever did anything nicer for a little girl than get her a drink of hot maple sirup right from the pan. Kathie, I'm sure, would agree. "When you're an old lady," I said, and a poem I read somewhere came to mind, "you can tell people that your father provided hot sirup for you."

So I got to wondering what some of our modern young people are going to have to remember when they get old. There are too many people growing up today who wouldn't know a maple from last year's woodpile, and I am speaking figuratively as well as specifically. When they get elderly, they'll have in their memories—what? I'm glad I had maple sugar time in my youth, and I'm sure Kathie, some day, will be glad too. I fancy I can hear her saying, pigtails gone and the years behind her, "When I was a little girl, every spring I used to go up in the woods with my father, and . . ."

1951
The Good Deed That Soured

The European aspects of the DP program had treatment here recently, and I am moved to tell how it worked on this end. All I know is this end, and it was a complete bust. If you run into some displaced DPs with canned milk for sale, tell them I was asking.

About two years ago our local Slovak parish priest lamented that he couldn't seem to get his flock interested in aiding DPs from their homeland. We have about 100 families of Slovak origin in town, and with hindsight I would now say they knew more than I did. But I told Father Edwin we would help if he so desired. He thought our proposition was valid.

Out on the knoll back of the buildings, by the pond, we have the log cabin we lived in for 15 years before we built our home. In Maine a log cabin is a sturdy dwelling, cozy and warm. Ours has hot and cold running water, electricity, and all necessary furnishings. A 4x6-foot picture window gives onto our valley, and we have always considered it a lovely view. Since we moved into the house we've stored apple crates, empty barrels, planters and such in the cabin, and it would take but an afternoon to make it ready for unfortunate friends from overseas.

Our proposition was merely that these friends would have an opportunity. We didn't want servants, and we have no need of hired help. If they wanted to begin life anew under more propitious circumstances, we could help them. They could have the cabin to live in; we would feed and clothe them until they got started; and we had no mercenary designs on them. They could use our farming equipment. I would buy them some cows and pigs. They could plant the fields. I could advise them, and they would have the counsel of other Slovaks in the area. We would charge off our expenses as a humanitarian contribution, and perhaps in five years—ten years—they could be ready to make a down payment on a farm of their own nearby.

Father Edwin communicated this to his church services, and this February we had word that a DP family was on the way. They had agreed to our proposition, and had certified themselves as willing to farm. We made the cabin ready, and Father Edwin went with us to meet them at the train.

I don't know what we were supposed to expect, but it was certainly our impression that these people would be destitute, that they had been driven by adversity so they would welcome a home, and that opportunity in this country would be gratifying to them. They were a nice-looking couple, and had a year-old daughter. The seven huge bundles of goods they unloaded from the train made us wonder at once.

The next day there came a trunk and a big wooden box, about four feet square, which four strong men could handle by grunting in chorus. Father Edwin had alerted his parishioners to be ready with gifts of clothing and food, and possibly household items we might neglect, but he saw at once his presumption of poverty was in error.

When the DPs unpacked, our cabin was a treasury of material wealth. The husband had an electric shaver far better than anything I can afford; a keen camera with every possible attachment; and a big radio that pulled in Russian stations so we could hear them all over the farm. The wife unpacked a beautiful electric iron. They had an intricate and aluminum baby buggy that collapsed to handbag size. And my wife eyed two rich fur coats the DP lady displayed proudly—nicer than anything I've been able to buy.

But we asked no questions and went ahead with our plans. Plain cow's milk wasn't good enough for the baby, so we bought a case of canned milk. We showed them our freezer, where they might help themselves to chickens; cuts of beef, pork and lamb; berries and vegetables; ice cream and fish. I took them down cellar and introduced them to apples, potatoes, turnips, cabbages, carrots, beets, maple sirup, onions, and a cask of vinegar. They said they preferred veal.

When we went to the store for our frugal weekly purchases, the DP lady picked up a cucumber, currently at 29¢. At 29¢, a cucumber is something we do without and wait patiently until the garden comes in. Observing our reluctance to buy this tidbit for their enjoyment, the DP lady said she would pay for it herself, which she did. The next day she flashed $20 bills at the stores until the clerks all thought I was crazy, and she bought $30 worth of things to send back to her parents in Europe.

I didn't know just how to take that. I didn't feel like paying grocery bills for people who could afford cucumbers and charity, but for the time being I let it go. There was a language difficulty, and I figured we could iron things out later.

Then they objected to the low condition of their existence, and said they had been far better off in Europe. The wife said they never had worn secondhand clothing, and they didn't intend to start now. The lovely baby things folks around town had brought in were merely an insult to them. I found donations of food in the hen pen.

So I telephoned Father Edwin and said I guessed another noble experiment had collapsed. I asked him to come find out what the score was, and if he felt things weren't hunky-dory to render into Slovak a little sentence I had composed, namely: "Git!"

He spent a whole afternoon talking with them, and concluded their intention had been to find an immediate excuse, any excuse, to move on to some prearranged destination other than our happy acres.

They admitted they were not farmers, and that they never had any intentions of farming. They had signed up as farmers because that was the only category that promised immediate entry to the United States. They said they never expected to stay here beyond three months, but would stay that long if I paid them $16 a day. In terms of the time of year, this was an exciting wage, because there is no gainful labor here between February and mid-May.

Father Edwin said he had conveyed my message. The DPs repacked, adding a number of local curios to their collection (including the case of canned milk), and at the railroad junction they plunked down the cash for sleeper accommodations to New York. I had paid their bills while they were here, but I hadn't given them a red cent in hand, and I would pay a pretty price to know where they got their funds.

They knew where they were going, all right, and they went. During the next few days a number of local Slovak people came and told me I was lucky to be shut of them. Evidently they knew something I didn't. Father Edwin and I both feel there is more to the story than we know.

I have put the planters, boxes, and barrels back in the cabin.

[Editor's Note—John Gould's experience points up the wisdom of more careful checking of incoming Displaced Persons, but should not be taken to reflect on the great majority of worthy DPs, countless numbers of whom are proving to be very welcome, contributive guests, friends, and neighbors throughout the United States.]

[This dispatch needs another footnote! Several months after it appeared in the *Monitor*, the secretary of the Roman Catholic bishop of Maine called me on the telephone to ask where my DPs might be. He sounded frantic. His church and the Friends had been joint sponsors of this displaced persons project and the United States government was now looking for our friends to deport them as unwanted foreign agents. I told him I had no idea where they went, but if I found out I'd be in touch at once. When our DPs sent us a card at Christmas, I telephoned the cathedral. Then, in turn, I got another Christmas card from the bishop, thanking me sincerely for extricating him from an embarrassing contretemps with the Federal Bureau of Investigation.—J. G.]

1952
Old-Fashioned Snowstorm

The slight delay in dispatching this intelligence comes from the fact that while no two snowflakes look alike, fifteen feet of them all piled up at once produces an impenetrable similarity, and I have been engaged in noticing this. I am reporting this for the benefit of folks who spent money to go South, for I want them to know they got their money's worth. They missed a lovely concentration that marooned us for three days, and I hope they appreciate it. I would not have missed it for doughnuts.

Some folks caught farther from home than we were may not agree, but I dare say they are already bragging about the ordeal, and take delight in making the snowstorm sound a good deal worse than it was. One crowd from here chartered a taxi to take them to the Ice Follies in Boston, and on the way home they spent two days in a farm kitchen, subsisting on saleratus biscuits, and they've made a nuisance of themselves ever since telling their friends about the great adventure.

I had nothing like that to set me apart, but I enjoyed the experience too. We were in no danger and had plenty of food and fuel.

We went down to the railroad junction to put the lad on the train so he could visit his grandparents in Boston, and the womenfolk just didn't get home that night. The family automobile gave up in a drift about a half mile from home, and we waded into a neighbor's to find three others had sought haven there before us.

About midnight I figured I was better off at home, so I left Mother and Kathie to spend the night on two chairs and walked up along the road. I breasted some snowdrifts worthy of respect, but got home with no trouble. Since then I have told how I floundered in circles, striking a light to read my compass, and generally emulating Peary in his dash to the Pole. The truth is that most of the two feet of snow fell after I made this walk. So I got home and undressed for bed.

Then the telephone rang, and it was the highway boss. He wanted to know if I had seen a snowplow. I said that I had not, but would be glad to observe one for him just as soon as he could arrange the schedule. He said things were pretty bad. Most of the trucks had broken pinions, warped camshafts, or moisture in the distributors.

One truck was down over a bank on Summer Street, and he wanted to locate another one for pulling-out purposes. He didn't know where the other one was, but in due time it ought to go by my place. He said this was the worst storm of his career, and the snow was coming faster than his trucks could clear it. He, himself, was now snowed in, and things looked bad all over.

I watched for this snowplow an hour or so, and then went to bed. The snowplow appeared at once. I got up again and snapped on the front light, going at once to the kitchen to break out an apple pie and bring the pot to boil. Around here the old mug-up custom is still observed, and a kitchen is a public place.

The snowplow ground to a stop out front and presently the crew came in. They said the roads were filling in behind them as fast as they punched through, and doubted very much if they could get over to Summer Street without having a pull or two themselves. We sat around and talked for a pie and a half, and then they drove off down the road and I went back to bed. At dawn the highway out front showed no signs of their having passed by, but the dirty dishes in the kitchen proved it was no dream.

The storm continued all the next day. After I got myself some breakfast and cleaned up the table I threw some high boots and warmer clothing into my packsack, took snowshoes and toboggan, and struck off to see how my two girl friends had made out. The highway was badly drifted, with places easily 15 feet deep, and in the howling northeast wind the walk was worse than it had been the night before.

But we came home together—Mother striding ahead on snowshoes and Kathie riding delightedly on the toboggan behind me. When we came to a big drift headed the right way, I would push her off over the edge, and she would slide real well.

After a time we caught up to Mother—she was standing on the precipice of a drift as blind as a bat, all ready to step off to her obvious doom. People who have experienced snow blindness will understand; others can imagine. So I led her home and dragged Kathie behind and we made it in due time.

Then we sat around and waited for the snowplow. It came two days later at 3:00 a.m., and instead of one of the town trucks it was a contractor's bulldozer weighing 19 tons. The crew came in for another mug-up and we were once more in contact with the outside world. We could go anywhere we wanted to, now. Even Florida.

But we haven't gone anywhere. We've stayed around home, enjoying the clean, white beauty of the surroundings, and for all the traveling we have in mind we might just as well be isolated still. Which seems to me to be material for a moral of some kind, but perhaps not worth the trouble. Anyway, we know that you can still be isolated by a Maine snowstorm, and that old-fashioned winters are still available from time to time. For a good many years, now, people have been going South to avoid winters that were more salubrious than what they went to, but this year they really missed a dandy. I'm glad I didn't.

1952
Strawberry Festival

Now the annual strawberry festival pours forth its gladness upon the scene, and everybody rejoices. I take part to the extent of my ability. I not only take part in the commercial or church vestry type upon any handy occasion, but I always hold one within the bosom of my family, and it is the best of the lot.

Some years back there was one regular strawberry festival in these parts. It had been going on for years in the Masonic Hall at Sou'West Bend and had a reputation. The menu was strawberry shortcake old-style, with strawberries and cream for dessert. People came for miles. But in more recent years the strawberry festival has become a general custom, and you can find one somewhere almost any evening during the season.

Last fall they even held one in September with frozen berries and it was declared a success. They planned it for strawberry time, but what with this and what with that they didn't get to hold it. So the committee popped the berries into the freezer and the delayed orgy was held at everybody's convenience.

Last year we went to several, and I was sorry to learn of the spreading acceptance of sweet-cake shortcake. I think I mentioned it at the time. I don't object to sweet cake as a foundation for strawberries, but I do think the definition of "shortcake" is too precise to permit such goings on. If they would advertise it as strawberry sweet cake I would accept it and go just the same, but I admire real shortcake and expect it to be as billed.

My own private strawberry festival is with wild strawberries, and I would like to put 1952 down as the best year yet. The wet spring was good for something after all, and rich, juicy straw-berries as big as acorns hang in the meadow grass. I've had my eye on them since we started the gardens. I can smell them.

The fields through which we go to the gardens took on a strawberry aroma, and I beagled around locating the spots. Until today I had brought up only a handful at a time, the first of which always goes to Mother because I enjoy her appropriate remarks concerning them. A handful of strawberries perks up a mother a good deal if delivered at the right time.

But there comes a day when the berries are ripe all over, and instead of picking them one at a time you can sweep up whole bunches, like flowers on a stem, and clean up a patch as you go. So I took a water pail and went at it. Nature has its own way of thinking things through, and the picking of whole stems is part of the plan. A pailful of ripe field strawberries would be mush in no time if you picked them separately. But with the stems attached, they are cushioned nicely. So the pailful came to the house unbruised, and it's easier to hull them if you gather stems and all.

I like to pick berries of any kind, but I think wild strawberries are best. Too many people remember the tediousness of it, and forget how fragrant the berries are in the grass—how they min-gle with the warmth of the sun on moist summer soil, and with the clover blooms and the rankness of thick herdsgrass. To pick wild strawberries is to be alone for a time in a maze of delight. People ten feet away couldn't have seen me, belly-bumps on the ground, hidden by the breeze-blown grass above. I like it.

We sat around the big kitchen table and tossed the hulled ber-ries into a common dish. This was nothing new—we'd been sit-ting around the table off and on for a week getting some cultivated strawberries ready for the freezer, hulling, cutting, sugaring, and packing in boxes. But no amount of tame berries will ever take the edge off wild ones. There is no comparison—they are truly two different fruits. This time the kitchen was full of the delicate, fragile, wistful fragrance of these wild ones, and our fingers were stained deep red with their just-ripe juices.

Our shortcake was made with buttermilk, which is about as high as you can go in the scheme of culture, and the old family recipe was used throughout. This makes an acre and a half, or three acres after you split and double-deck it. It calls for the big platter, the one on which a twenty-pound turkey at Thanksgiving always looks like a starved squab.

One thing I deplore is the commercial notion that skimping on strawberries is all right if you cover a shortcake's modesty with whipped cream. A tiara of stabilized whipped cream, adorned with a whole berry, does not compensate for a frugal serving underneath. To keep serving people honest, I insist that shortcakes on my table arrive in full view of the participants. Cream may then be added if desired. It is hard to skimp that way, and mine is a good rule. So we pile the strawberries on until the big platter buckles with the weight, and then overlay the top part and repeat. In this way nothing detracts from the main idea.

Then we eat it.

This is a strawberry festival. And after I have celebrated sufficiently I have a dish of wild strawberries, a slice of homemade bread and butter, and a glass of milk before going to bed. I sleep well, and thus we pass the time in our uncouth, bucolic way.

1953
Ice-Taking vs. Ice-Making

Kennebago Lake, which is in the minor civil division known as "Township 3, Range 4, West of Bingham's Kennebec Purchase," has joined the growing list of "Great Ponds" in Maine which are no longer cutting ice in the bleak January frigidity. I learned this the other day during a short but pleasant conversation with Bud Russell, who operates the old summer hotel (or "camps") in that remote region.

Bud said he'd bought an ice-making machine. Kennebago was one of the first places in Maine to discover the "tourist" business, and people have been going there for a long time to enjoy the summer season.

None of the seasonal guests has ever seen the same lovely land and lakescape, naturally, in the time for cutting ice, when a hardy gang of thick-clothed woodsmen gather to fill the big icehouse behind the dingle. Right now some seven or eight feet of snow dominate the scene, and about three feet of ice would be found on top of the lake.

For close to a hundred years the program has been to send in some supplies and a cook, break out the long woodroad, clear away the snow, and hoist the big cakes of ice into the house. Then sawdust is used for insulation, and in about a week the deed is done. Everybody goes back out to town, and nobody ventures into the region again until mid-May when the first queries begin to come about rates and reservations from city-weary rusticators.

I'm using Kennebago something as a symbol. The ice-making

machine seems like a needless expense in a region where the winter descends early and has nothing to do for five months except make ice that is free for the taking. And by "free for the taking" I am stating an early and immutable principle of Maine law.

Back when the founding fathers set up the rules by which we live, they established the "Great Pond Law." This asserts a public, and common, ownership of certain resources. Some of the rights and privileges have since been finagled astutely by less-than-good politicians, and there is, today, a subtle distinction between fact and theory. But one of the rights that nobody can deny is the public ownership of ice. Any inhabitant of Maine can go to any body of water over ten acres and cut himself some ice.

It doesn't make any difference what real estate possessiveness has accrued since the state was founded, the access to ice-cutting is basic, inherent, and unquestioned. You will find the right specifically stated in our earliest laws, and during all these years no repeal, amendment, or curtailment has prevailed.

If you want to cut some ice, a "No Trespassing" sign needn't bother you a bit. Shall I add, "In theory"? Because, as ice-cutting has declined in general, there might be some need of establishing your right to the ponds in some places. When something lapses, it's always harder to revive it.

Anyway, when Bud told me he'd bought an ice-making machine, it pointed up the lapse. Bud says the machine cost him less than the bill for two years' ice harvesting, not counting the expense of digging the ice out come summer. And thus, of course, another ancient privilege of the people passes into desuetude—rendered obsolete by the advancements of mechanics.

One of my first jobs was on a pond, helping to harvest ice. I had a long pole with a hook, and I would drag the strips of ice through the open water to the runway into the icehouse. A man stood there with a needlebar and broke the strips up into cakes, and then horses worked the cables that elevated them for storage. One time we worked three days running and never saw the thermometer above − 25, but Ralph Prout was tiering the cakes in his undershirt. So, I am not lamenting the lapse of ice-cutting for any sentimental love of the job.

Later, one summer, I earned college money by peddling ice around town. With tongs and a rubber shoulder cape I would totter from icebox to icebox, and on Wednesday afternoons we filled the market meatboxes with blocks and tackles. Some of them took a whole load. A typical memory concerns staggering up three flights of stairs to an icechest on an outside porch, where an elderly lady preserved her perishables by padding a ten-cent piece with newspapers.

I was wiry, but not rugged, and a ten-cent piece in those days would run to at least 50 pounds of ice. The lady would survey the piece that had all but keeled me over in my ascent and complain, "That's awfully small for a ten-center!" She reported me as an upstart to my boss, the owner of the business, after I told her, "Look, Ma'am, you lug it upstairs once and it'll seem a lot bigger." I can't say I relinquished my position with regrets. I won't say the general subject of ice makes me sigh for a lost cause.

But I was sorry to learn that one more of the great ponds had been sacrificed, and one more of our "unalienable rights" was thus weakened and rendered less demonstrable. There may, indeed, come a time when somebody will want to cut ice, and somebody else will say, "Thou shalt not!" This would be contrary to the ancient precepts, but it wouldn't be so very different from a lot of other things that have slipped away.

1954
A Duck and a Lesson in Communism

Ducks continue to teach valuable lessons, and I will not apologize for returning to the subject. The duck that thought he was a sheep, recently described here, still thinks so. Not long ago my brother-in-law shifted his sheep from their home territory to a summer range up on the hill, but the duck who lived with them so cozily was not moved. The duck who baa-ed was left behind.

He immediately went into a decline. He ran all about the first day looking everywhere to see what had happened to his relatives. He trotted all over. When he couldn't find them he would come up to the house and tell everybody all about it. The family sympathized deeply, but this testimony of concern did not assuage the duck's inconsolable anxiety. He finally gave up and sulked. He crawled in under the shed and made himself miserable. Now and then a plaintive baa could be heard.

He stayed there three days.

Finally they had to send little Willie in under the shed, because he was the only person small enough to make it, and Willie came dragging the sad duck out by the neck (which is the proper way to grasp a duck, you know) and they clapped the duck in a box and drove up on the hill with him. They released him on the edge of the field, and he waddled up amongst the flock of sheep with many a glad cry of recognition, and is happy again.

I can substantiate this story with reputable witnesses, and can even show you the duck, living with the sheep and thinking he is one of them. I think the significance, as I see it, lies in this proof that you can adjust to about anything if you just put your mind to it and aren't fussy.

Speaking of ducks, I have just had a good lesson in communism. Two of my mallards went a-setting this spring, and the only thing unusual was that they chose the same spot. With about 150 acres here, they decided to occupy the same space at the same time, and when I found them they had 17 eggs. They were sitting side by side, looking as if they weren't there at all, as mallards can, and sharing the work-load in good style.

A mallard nest is interesting. The mallard is a wild bird, but can be domesticated. None of the other web-footed friends domesticate worth a cent—meaning the blacks, teal, ruddies, canvasbacks, etc. You can start black ducks in your barnyard, but come fall they'll fly. The mallard, however, gets to like people. So you have the chance to watch a really wild bird under tame conditions. I waited a day or two after I first discovered their hidden nest, and when they were over at the feed hopper I sneaked around and counted the eggs. The nest was completely hidden while the birds were away, dried grass covering the spot. Down under the grass, carefully wrapped in down, were the 17 eggs. And about a week after that the two ducks showed up in the pond with 17 little ducks, about as big as bumblebees and almost the same color.

Then the fun began. The contemplative and theoretical aspects of communism, so easy to accept during the ruminative weeks of incubation, struck a snag in the light of possessive, inherent instincts which came to the fore as the burdens of motherhood closed in. Each duck, who had willingly shared the comtemplative portion of the arrangement, now got the idea that all 17 ducklings were hers. It looked to me like the disintegration of the whole philosophy, a bust-up of the motivating dream—the clash of idealistic experiment with the practicalities of private ownership. It precipitated a great big fight, which went on and on.

The ducklings were no great help. Nurtured in a common nest, they didn't know which was which. They didn't even care—they would huddle now under one and now under the other. But, being ducks, they did not try to huddle under both at once. The Communist, I suppose, would argue that each mother should take 8½ ducks. Ducks don't operate that way. The whole 17 would huddle under one duck a while, and then all 17 would go over and huddle under the other. Every time they were under one duck, the other duck would butt in and make trouble. The little ducks got stepped on quite a bit, and peeped about it, and I figured it was time to do something. I hated to intrude into a great social experiment like this, but I could see the philosophy was in trouble.

My solution was a forthright capitalistic trick. I grabbed one duck by the neck and stuck her under an apple crate, where she sat for three days and called me names. The other duck took the 17 children and began rearing them without competition.

The duck under the box got over it, and when I turned her loose she went off on the pond with the drake and paid no further attention to the babies, which is what I thought she would do. A great many ideological posers will resolve themselves if you stop thinking about them.

The ordinary clutch of ducklings, for mallards, runs to seven or eight. Seventeen is more than one mother can easily cover. To see this bird stretch herself and brood all 17 is a great lesson in what a person can do if he extends himself.

When the little ducks are all under her, and she is dozing in the sun, I like to sneak up and make a noise like a foreign power. Alarmed, the 17 babies leap to their feet, rush to the water, and carry their mother bodily with them. She makes her feet go, without touching the ground, and talks a great deal, and seems to think this is not exactly the outcome she expected. This, too, might be a lesson for us.

1954
In the Yankee Manner

Yankee Hospitality is another matter, and any evidence on the subject should be appreciated. Here, then, is the illuminating story of a Southern Gentleman who was touring Maine with his wife and two children in a new-model station wagon.

I guess they were all over before they left, but on this particular morning they had passed over a rock in the road. This was a large rock whose other end was attached to the State of Maine, and there was a crunch and a jingle. They gazed behind to see their muffler and exhaust pipe expiring upon the road, near said rock.

Now their fine automobile sounded like a flight of jet planes, which is not only against the law for automobiles (although they don't do anything about jet planes) but is not the best kind of a noise to tour by. They came down out of the mountains into a smallish village about nine a.m., and sought a garage.

The Southern Gentleman had meantime been priming his family. "This," he said, "is where we take a sticking. These backcountry Yankee characters know all the ways to take us. We are in an alien land, among sharpies and carpetbaggers. They'll skin the eyeteeth out of your head and you looking at them. We've had bad luck, and we might as well grin and bear it. We're about to be run through the grinder. I suppose this will be the most expensive tailpipe ever attached. . . ."

And so on. Thus they came to a combination filling station, general store, garage, souvenir shop, films developed, and ice cream parlor. The lanky, emaciated character who was tilted back on a straight-legged chair, his hat adorned with fishing flies, got up at the noise and walked over. He glanced at the out-of-state license plate and said, "Don't that thing have any muffler?"

"It did have, but we hit a rock. Have you one that will fit this car?"

"I dunno."

"Don't you repair cars?"

"Eyuh."

"Well, I'd like a new muffler."

"I sh'd think you would."

"Have you got one?"

"Guess not."

"Don't you have any mufflers on hand?"

"Eyuh."

"Well, let's look and see if you've got one for me."

"Nope."

"What do you mean, nope?"

"I mean I'm not going to put on any muffler today."

"Why not, aren't you in that business?"

"Yes, I'm in business all right. Too much in business. I got so much business I don't have time for anything else. I got nobody to tend these pumps, and if I ever got under your car I'd have a flurry of business, and I'd be up and down, up and down, and I just don't feel like it. You can get a muffler down to Waterville, or Augusta."

"But I don't feel like driving all that noise as far as Waterville. I'll tend the pumps for you; I can pump gas. Let's see if you've got a muffler my size."

The Southern Gentleman went into the shed beside the store and found a good assortment of tailpipe assemblies, one of which fit his automobile. He came carrying it out, and the Yankee Character was tilted back on the chair again. The conversation that ensued was lengthy, and the Southern Gentleman assumed that every word he spoke was effectively jacking up the price of the final settlement. But he had made up his mind to a sticking, and the progress towards it was incidental. He at last prevailed on the garageman to crawl under and start work.

Immediately there was a flurry of business. So the Southern Gentleman pumped gasoline and wiped windshields and kept busy. The morning ran along. The garageman under the car had occasional remarks about this and that, mostly to himself, and he made it clear he was not happy about anything. He spoke a good deal about tourists who came along and upset his program.

But the job got done and the garageman said, "There!" They started the motor, and it purred like a kitten.

Taking a deep breath, the Southern Gentleman asked the vital question, "How much?"

"Well, I dunno. I'd have to look it up."

Then followed a rest period in which the Southern Gentleman thought the garageman was going to look it up, but during which the garageman didn't do anything.

"Aren't you going to look it up?"

"What's your hurry? You seem to be all drove up. Why don't you calm down and enjoy life? You came two thousand miles to see me, and now you want to rush off."

"Well, yes . . . but, you see. . . ."

"But, nothing!"

Finally he looked it up. "I got those mufflers secondhand, sort of. I bought fifty of them from a fellow failed up down to Hartland. I didn't pay full price. It cost me, let's see . . . two-nineteen, and I paid two dollars to get them trucked over here. That's four cents, ain't it? Well, two-nineteen and four, that's two-twenty-three. Two-twenty-three you owe me."

"Two-twenty-three? Why . . . that's not enough. You can't put a tailpipe on a car for two-twenty-three! You got your labor to figure in, and some kind of a profit! Why . . ."

". . . Now look—you-all! I didn't want to do business with you in the first place. I was all cocked and primed for a lazy day. I didn't want to do a thing, all day. You came blowing in here like the end of the world, and you insisted I go to work. Tomorrow, yesterday—it would'a been different. But today I didn't want you around. You're a nuisance today. So give me two-twenty-three, and that's all I want."

"But the labor. . . ."

"The labor is mine, and I can put a price on it or not, just as I please. Now give me two-twenty-three and get out of here."

The Southern Gentleman counted out two one dollar bills, two dimes and three cents, handed them over, and drove away in a magnificent silence.

1955
Heidi vs. Hie-di-hi

Heidi is now Hie-di-hi, and e'en hie-di-ho. Kathy announced recently that Heidi would be telecast and her childhood wouldn't be complete unless she might see this spectacle. So I made arrangements, and we went over to spend the evening with a wealthy neighbor who has a television set, but who had never heard of Heidi before, and he was delighted to oblige us.

I wanted to see it myself. I've had to relive the childhood books twice, and although I don't really think it's as good a book as Joe Strong, the Boy Fish, Heidi is one of those things you have to go along with. It's a tear-jerker, but its underlying philosophy is sound. Grandfather Heidi, seemed to me, was the real character in the thing, living like a Swiss Thoreau, knowledgeable and aware, rightly dividing things as he knew them. Everything comes out right, and little Heidi remains in your thoughts.

But the thing was a disappointment when the opening remarks revealed the all-wise American television and advertising fraternity had decided to produce Heidi as a musical. I have no quarrel with the musical idea in the aggregate, but I seldom like the way specific pieces turn out, and it was impossible to maintain a mood when full orchestras unexpectedly blared from out the edelweiss-festooned vistas of the remote and unfrequented Helvetian Alps, just because somebody decided to sing. But that wasn't all.

Our friend, thinking Heidi must be something extremely wonderful to bring us two over to his place, prepared to enjoy it with open mind. He knew it wasn't going to be a wrestling match or a quiz show, but otherwise he was unprepared. Then he went off into uncontrolled hysterics when Grandfather Heidi, already well-tagged as a bucolic expert, picked up a Snow & Neally double-bitted ax and began to split some wood. He gave the tool about seventeen flourishes as yet unknown to the lumbering industry, and sank the blade into the side of the stick.

Since the double-bitted ax is a chopping tool, this dramatic act would result in some delay as the 57 varieties of television assistant producers gathered to withdraw the ax, which they couldn't possibly do in time for the play to finish on schedule. Yet Grandfather Heidi brought it up without effort and struck again. After considerable striking it was revealed that he had successfully split one stick into two pieces, a veritable miracle, and he picked these two pieces up and walked to his hut as if he had the fuel problem licked for another long, mountain winter.

My friend continued to laugh about this up to the time they began making cheese in a churn, said churn being an early American model sometimes known as a Walpole Exerciser, and often called worse than that by the unfortunate pioneers who tried to make butter in them. I could see that my friend was enjoying Heidi a great deal.

It seems to me two rather good points can be made. The first is somewhat intangible, having to do with the smug superiority of American television, which thinks a story like Heidi can be improved. We run into this attitude often, and it is always irking to sensitive folks.

I knew a schoolteacher poet once who was rewriting the Psalms. Some of the Psalms, presumably, might be bettered here and there—but that isn't the point. The point is that the Psalms were left by their writer in a certain form, and he wrote them that way because that was his genius and his expression. To translate the Psalms from one language to another is another kind of genius and expression, but honest labor requires that as much as possible of the original be retained and brought over. If you don't like what was first written, I presume you have the right to start fresh and write some Psalms of your own, but they should be your own, and not "rewrites."

To arrange Heidi for dramatic presentation, or even for a musical, lies within the province of art, just as translation does, but you should still seek to keep the motivating purpose, the tone, the style, and even the personalities of the original. Otherwise you shouldn't call it Heidi. Otherwise you should write your own play.

But that point is elusive and Americans will readily remind us that any approach is justified if it sells automobiles. The second point is more in my line—and has to do with axes and such. I should like to hire out as an advisory expert, at a modest fee, to inform and instruct television directors in matters rural. Since all television shows seem to originate in urban surroundings, and at least 98 per cent of them have one rural sequence, the industry's efforts toward verisimilitude lead to technical lapses which detract from the story purposes. My friend based his entire appraisal of Heidi on an ax.

Somebody needs to tell television people that pine limbs,

draped before a camera, are not fir. Somebody needs to stave off the lovely heroine who, at a moving moment, sniffs a daisy and indicates pleasure at the flavor. Daisies don't have that kind of a smell. Somebody needs to tell the historical delvers that you don't drive New England oxen with a horsewhip, or shout giddap at them. And a halibut is a hawlibut.

Shakespeare said it—that you must keep your audience from wandering off the important business at hand; that while a crucial dramatic effect is being gained you must avoid misleading people. In short, you mustn't come up with the wrong ax at the right time.

Anyway, Kathy said the book was a good deal better than the television show, and Kathy is a fair critic. She thought Heidi was much too old, and when I explained that it took an older, trained voice to sing the part, Kathie said she didn't think the singing added anything.

1956
An Item for Curio-Hunters

When my recent concrete work had progressed to a gratifying conclusion, I had maybe a half-pail of mixed-up concoction left over, and the question came on what to do with it. The stuff begins to set up and harden shortly, and when rigid is in a fairly permanent state, so wet cement is something you should decide about right then and there.

I finally smoothed it out over a patted-down patch of gravel, so it makes a steppingstone, and there it is to this very day. If I ever need a steppingstone, I can go right there and get it. But somewhere along the line I bemusedly considered the wonderful chance I had to manufacture a hitching weight.

There's an item the present-day curio-hunters haven't adapted to their special purposes. The wagon wheels adorn the driveway; old butter molds look cute on the whatnot; churns can be filled with petunias; and flatirons will hold open a door. But the hitching weight, seems to me, has not turned up in a new and improved place, to show that contemporary living retains great love of the educational past. Somebody might turn his mind to this and do us all a great favor, for I'm sure the countryside is still well stocked with hitching weights that can be picked up for a song.

The hitching weight, original model, was only a stone or metal anchor for a horse. It would be about as big around as a pork pie, with a ring of some sort where you attached the rope or leather line that connected said weight to the horse's bridle. This gave you a portable mooring for Dobbin, which you carried in the buggy under the seat until occasion demanded it.

I suppose somebody had a business making these things, for they came cast from iron or shaped from granite. You could also get some made from cement, but a farmer could make himself one of that kind by filling a pan with the dab of cement left over from some job, and setting an eyebolt into it. Outboard motor enthusiasts make the same sort of weight today for killicks, using a gallon can.

You didn't "park" a horse; you stood him. And few horses in these parts were well enough trained so they'd stand any length of time. You might trust them long enough to run in and get a package of pickling spice, but if you left them much longer than that you could well return to find the conveyance homeward-bound without you.

Makes me think of the fellow up country who wasn't too rugged in the head, but whose muscles were tremendous. Lacking a pair, one time, they hitched him in with an odd steer and used him for plowing. He worked very well, geeing and hawing on command and requiring very little prodding with the goad, and they ripped up sodground all forenoon until a bee stung him and he ran away.

O'er hill and dale, the plow bobbing around in the air, he and the steer cavorted at top speed, until they were cornered up by the woods, all tangled in the yoke and chain until it was necessary to unhitch and hitch again. At this point the old fellow said, "Unyoke the steer! I'll stand!"

Hitching posts, the basic forerunner of the parking meter, were spaced along the sidewalks of the village, but on rainy days when farmers came to town it might be hard to find a free space, so the hitching weight was under the seat if you needed it. You plopped it on the ground, snapped the line to the ring of the bit, and your horse was tethered. It took a strong-mouthed horse to move such a weight.

Farmers were no different from modern motorists who think they should have parking space when they come to spend money, so if you had to get out your hitching weight it was a reflection on the businessmen who solicited your trade—they should have provided more hitching posts.

Back about the time automobiles were changing our lives one of the local merchants built a new store, equipped it handsomely, laid in a big stock, and held a grand opening. Grandfather went around to look the place over. The proprietor, pleased, came up rubbing his hands and said, "Well, Tom, what do you think of it?"

Tom said it was a lavish display and a fine job, but added, "You won't last a year." The storekeeper huffed a little at that, but Gramp's judgment often worked out, so he said, "What makes you say that?"

Gramp said, "You got no place out front to hitch a horse."

It proved to be so. Farmers went on down the street where they could hitch, and the brand-new store sold out at a sacrifice after ten months. The storekeeper acknowledged Gramp's forecast, too. Right after that automobiles moved in and the order changed. Horses were relegated to antiquity and the hitching post was no longer a factor in retail economy.

The same store is there today and doing all right, but that change in ownership was the dividing line between two eras. So the hitching post and the hitching weight had their day and we moved along, and that's the way it was.

This has nothing to do with hitching weights, but right after that store was opened, about the time Gramp made his gloomy forecast, Jim Norton went in one day with an egg and asked if he could swap it for a darning needle. Jim was kind of a tight-fisted fellow and got along with as little money as anybody. The storekeeper said he would, so the swap was made, and as Jim walked toward the door he noticed the new soda fountain—quite a novelty in those days.

"My, my," he said. "Ain't she beautiful! Don't that call for a free sody on the house?"

The storekeeper grinned, knowing Jim well enough, and walked around behind the fountain with the egg still in his hand. "All right," he said. "What'll you have?"

Jim said, "Anything with an egg in it."

So the storekeeper reached for a bottle of milk, and cracked the egg into a glass. It turned out to be a double-yolker.

"Aha!" said Jim. "You owe me another darning needle!"

1957
A Winter Storm in
Retrospect

"If it snows much more," said Kathie, "we won't have any school tomorrow." The joyful anticipation of such a holiday confuses me—you'd think with the bigger and better bond issues the finer and fuller program would have promoted considerable eagerness. It seems not to be so. "The bus had all it could do to get up the hill tonight," she said.

In the continuing dispute over then and now, the severity of weather in former times seems to win, possibly because the old-timers shout louder, but truth-to-tell we didn't very often have a storm that stopped school.

Another thing that complicates comparisons is the tendency to remember specific storms, instead of weather in general, and Kathie's remark led me to do just that. It was a storm we had in 1920 that came to mind—one that filled in the countryside and brought things to a halt. The snow was so deep the horses couldn't get around to "break the roads"; it plugged up a train so it stood three days; and it filled in our cross-country electric tracks so we had no trolleys for weeks. They finally let out the shoe factories so the men could shovel and get the cars going again. All the rest of the winter the trolleys ran down in a ravine with places fixed so passengers could go down on steps to get aboard.

This storm was northeasterly, and began about ten o'clock in the morning while we were all at school. At noontime the village youngsters got home to dinner all right, and came back bundled and scarfed for the afternoon session. But when things let out for the day we trudged off in snow that was hip-deep and swirling in a bitter wind.

I broke a path for the Pendleton girls. They lived above us on the road, and when I came to my driveway I went right on, with the Pendleton girls wading behind Indian file, heads down and nobody talking. Then I backtracked, and the storm had already filled in our path.

Mother had gone out to throw scratch-grain to my hens and pick up the eggs, because the storm brought darkness early that night, so I didn't have to do that. I had my supper, and passed the usual winter evening at home with grammar and arithmetic, popcorn and apples, and a pitch game with Uncle. Then I took my kerosene lamp and headed for my attic room. The house was wired for electricity, but they hadn't run a circuit up into the attic, so I worked off coal-oil. The little room had sloping ceilings, under the roof, and red roses on the wallpaper. The one single-sash window faced northeast by east, and had to be taken out of the casing if I wanted air.

It was a wonderful boy's room, away up above the affairs of the family, but uninhabitable by the newer standards of comfort. It was hotter than a sawmill engine all summer, and worse than Greenland's icy mountains all winter. But I made out, and always thought I had the best room in the house.

A winter storm in that room was a magnificent experience, and this one I speak of topped them all. I didn't open my window, of course, and it rattled all night in the casing. The thin plaster and the flowery wallpaper had no insulation qualities whatever, and beyond them were the pine roofers, the cedar shingles, and winter. My head was ten inches below that.

I was warm in bed after I got there and stopped quaking. Speed was a great thing. It was no joke that a boy could blow out his lamp and be under the covers before it got dark. The only heat in that bedroom was what I made myself by coiling up in a ball under the comfortables and blankets.

I remember how the rafters creaked that night from the wind, and how the storm sounded like sandpaper on the shingles, as the wind whipped the stinging particles against the roof. But I slept all right, and it was still snowing when Mother opened the door at the foot of the attic stairs and called, "Hurry—it's the most wonderful morning you ever saw, more snow than you ever heard of, and still coming!"

I remember this pleased me. It was fun to have a lot of snow. My clothes were well cooled down and I got them on in the usual nothing-flat. Downstairs Mother had the kitchen light on, because snow covered the windows. "You'll have to hurry," she said. "It will take longer to get to school this morning."

It did. I was really late, except that I fell in with the teacher at the post office, and she was late too, so she couldn't very well call anybody tardy. It snowed that day until mid-afternoon, and I'm sure if we'd had buses then we'd never have got home. We heard that a train was stalled on the main line, and they'd have to shovel 800 yards of track to get a snowplow through. Some people thought the trolleys wouldn't run again until spring. On the roads they went out around big drifts, right over fences.

Neal Fitts made his expected witticism: "Wore out two snow-shovels, I did, right down to the nubs, just getting to the shed." And the old timers were all saying that while this was a fair storm, it was nothing compared to what they used to have.

1957
"Delineator of Nature"

To The Christian Science Monitor:
A difference of opinion seems to exist regarding John Gould's qualifications as a humorist. Until recently I had assumed that *Monitor* readers were unanimous in their appreciation of his salty, down-to-earth sallies. No matter what the subject, if it just happens to fall across John's path, it seems good for a column in the *Monitor*.

For years my family and many friends have enjoyed him, fitting emotion to emotion, and wishing, like Mr. Harry White of Hillsboro, Ore., that we might some day drop in on our friend at Lisbon Falls and tell him of our gratitude for his weekly grist. So one day a little while ago we took the whole family up and around "the winding rise" and knocked on the old homestead door. John's wonderful wife, so cordial in her welcome to strangers, said John was gathering blueberries just over the knoll and she was sure he would be along soon as it was nearly noon.

He came promptly on time for a milk and bread 'n' butter lunch and we, having had our noon bite, just sat and visited. Reminded us of descriptions of young Mr. Lincoln of Illinois—he was so full of practical common sense and sparkling good humor. We didn't stay too long—not nearly as long as we would have liked. John recommended that we see more of his beloved Maine, and directed us up to the Lake Mooselookmeguntic area, a parting suggestion we have always since appreciated.

John Gould is more than a wit, more than a humorist. He is a delineator of nature, human and otherwise, seldom equaled and never excelled. Our nation needs more John Goulds.

James K. Westover

Buffalo, N.Y.

1958
A Word with a Wallop

W hen the big-shot government attorneys were up here in Maine last spring to prosecute Maine lobstermen for organizing to get better prices, an unimportant but interesting word crept into the testimony. Fortunately the presiding justice, who has been in touch with down-East affairs from boyhood, knew the word and the proceedings were able to continue.

There was testimony to indicate that something of a scuffle had arisen at one time between two of the fishermen—a difference of opinion of an advanced nature, which resulted in something of a bodily onset and was finally broken up by fifteen rugged neighbors and the State Police. The government attorneys, to emphasize the great disturbance this price question had insinuated in an otherwise peaceful domestic era, made quite a bit of this and drew the gory details out to a fine point.

Of course, the Washington attorneys, mostly devoting their careers to large combines and industrial trusts, were at a disadvantage from the beginning, for if any great truth prevails in this world it is that you don't be down-East unless you are down-East, and the life, language, actions, interests, and habits of these top-notch individuals of the Maine coast cannot be assimilated, understood, and appreciated by nonresident tendencies.

It was therefore immediately amusing to many that this alter-cation, even when it got into the category of peen hammers and boathooks, was only a friendly discussion, and its cause, pur-pose, and outcome had no particular significance, and certainly no esoteric values worth all the prying and prodding. Not knowing this, the attorneys pounded away at it, and after firmly establishing that there had been one old rauncher of a fight, they released the witness for examination by the defense.

The defense lawyer, himself a waterside product, came for-ward with a gentle smile on his lips, leaned on the rail, and in a friendly and proper manner asked, "That was quite a fight you had with him, wasn't it?"

The witness, clearly pleased, said, "Eyuh, 'twas."

"But," said the lawyer, "you weren't mad at him, were you?"

Now comes the word referred to.

The witness said, "Daow!"

The transcript of the day's hearing was priced at $50, a sum beyond the abilities of the poor fishermen, and also beyond me, and I do not know how the court reporter wrote it down. The government attorneys, unrestricted in their expenditures, all had copies, and so did their assistants and supporters, but I was not of a mind to approach them. I have spelled it "daow" because that is the nearest I can come.

The witness meant, by the use of this word, the facial expres-sion he took on, and the tone of his voice, that the question was utterly ridiculous to begin with, and a sensible person would never have asked it. Furthermore, that the idea behind the ques-tion, that ill-feeling had prevailed, was equally absurd, and that only the lowest mentality would ever think of it, even. It dis-missed immediately the entire premise of the government attor-neys, evaporating their inferences.

Most significant of all, the word expressed infinitely more than could ever be said by a plain no, even if drawn out to sev-eral syllables.

This word is in Maine speech, but is not heard every day. It is, properly, an expanded no. It is called in when a plain no is inadequate. It follows a question which would never call for a yes, and which is too foolish to be simply denied. I saw Winnie Raymond along in August, and asked, "Are you getting any tomatoes?"

Winnie said, "Daow!"

True, Winnie gave me a no answer, but he also criticized the entire growing season, with reference to undue rains, continued west to northerly winds of a cool nature, and the ineffectiveness of what sunlight we had, plus an assessment of my general intelligence in presuming that anybody's tomato plants had fructified to that extent.

Furthermore, Winnie indicated, thus, that the subject was of no interest to him any more, that the garden had been crossed off as a great waste of time, and that he would prefer to indulge some other, less unhappy, topic. I do not know how, in any language or dialect, you could get any more into one word.

From time to time, as I ruminate on such peculiarities of conversation, I wonder about the dictionary makers. I am told it took 35 years to get the word "zut!" past the French Academy and into the dictionary, and that it still lacks a precise and communicable definition. It is one of those things which convey everything when intoned in context and accompanied by proper gestures.

Daow is such a word, and although I have heard it well over 35 years now, I am confident it will not soon appear in the book. It has, however, appeared in federal court, and momentarily halted all progress while a batch of high-priced bureaucratic attorneys looked bewildered and unhinged.

The poor lobstermen were found guilty, although everybody here felt the law was faultily drawn and had never been meant to pick on them this way. To some, the high spot of the whole trial was the daow. It answered the question, and the whole indictment.

1959
Sweet Sixteen in Beantown

Well, Congress convened, and some Russian passed our way, and we have a banner with a strange device, and they tell me the sun has been assaulted—but in a family that attains a 16-year-old daughter such news is looked at askance, if at all. She had her party, with everybody in, and considerable acknowledgment was made. Sweet Sixteen having special significance, whatever it is, my annual dinner for two was increased accordingly.

Since she was old enough to know me from somebody else, I've made a fatherly custom of two stated convocations involving nobody else. Every June she and I strike out on some wilderness jaunt—we view the trout chowder in its native lair, follow some back trail to new delights, broil a couple of steaks in some picturesque dell, and enhance the day with our mutual conversations. Then, every January, we doll all up and go out to some elite victualer's, throwing caution to the winds and having the expensive one.

It started without any particular plan. The first year we made our hike I had to carry her some, and the principal reward was a snatch of moccasin flowers. But each year the experiences expanded. When she was maybe seven she went swimming while I fried the trout, and she gashed her knee on a sharp, underwater rock. She didn't tell me of this until after we'd eaten, because she didn't want to delay the fun.

When she was eight she was fly-casting in a pool, and two men, garbed from the city shops and hung with expensive equipment, came along, watched her, and asked her to show them the trick of underarm loop casting, which she was doing because of the bushes. She showed them, and then gave them her trout, because they hadn't been able to catch any.

The January outings have similarly developed. One year, a ribbon jaunty on her long hair, she informed the waitress and everybody else in earshot that the lobster was not cooked "the way my mom cooks it!" It wasn't. Then once, at the happily remembered old Mansion House at Poland Spring, I paid the long price for the full dinner, and she sat for an hour-and-a-half and ate peanut butter and crackers. "Some birthday!" said the waitress. But she ordered for herself, and it was her party.

This year I happened to have an errand in downtown Boston, so I thought I'd lengthen the event. I called her at five a.m., "Come on, I want to show you the teakittle in Scollay Square!"

It was still dark, and although the sun was to come up red it shortly went behind clouds, and the day was chill. We had no traffic to fight, and with the new roads we can approach Boston in less than three hours. It wasn't long ago we had to allow at least six, and if you had a flat or the beach crowd was out, it took more. So we were at Sullivan Square in Charlestown by the time folks were stirring, and we left the automobile and headed for the elevated.

The man in the booth, when we bought some tokens, was early-morning alert, for he leaned ahead and said, "Are you under-age?"

She said, "No, sir." I smiled, for "sir" is not rightly in our down-East lingo, and we seldom use it. Not to a man in a change booth, anyway—and no slight intended. It's a formality more common to non-Mainers.

She was disgusted. Anybody ought to see she was sixteen!

"Gee," she said later. "I could-a-ridden cheaper, and he'd never known the diff!"

"No," I said with fatherly philosophy, and a desire to inculcate the ethics. "No, he'd never have known—but you would."

"Yeh, that's right."

We didn't do anything much. We spoke of how glum and sour everybody looked. Nobody speaking; nobody smiling. An elevated crowd is so aloof. Around home, everybody speaks and smiles in the morning. "What do you suppose that woman would do if I walked up and spoke to her?" she asked.

"She'd break out in a smile, and be as friendly as long underwear, and remember you all her life," I said, but I don't know if this is true. She said, "I guess they just don't know how."

I took her into the Parker House and showed her the ornamental fireplaces her great-great-uncle, who was a mason, laid up when he was a young man, and which have been studied many times by apprentices as beautiful and intricate construction. We spoke to a couple of ear-muffed policemen, who seemed glad to see us, and looked in store windows, and investigated several propositions which seemed worth it at the time, but probably pass in Boston as ordinaries.

I did my errand, and we did see the teakittle (although it has cooled down and I had stressed the steam from it) and we sat on some stools and ate some dry sandwiches which the lunch man probably had left over from the celebration in 1930.

We got a look at those hallowed artifacts in the vicinity, the burial grounds and the subway ventilators, the chapel and the church, the out-of-town newspaperman, the statehouse and Faneuil Hall, and the place that matches any coat with new pants. I have an idea our casual enjoyment encountered many things Bostonians haven't noticed in years, and I had to remind her that the errand of the day had kept us in but a small section of the city, and had limited our field.

"Can we go home now?" she asked.

That sounded good to me, so we went in the hole and rode back to our automobile, and in the gathering dusk of a cold winter birthday we set sail for the distant glimmer of warm lamplight in the clearing, and left Olde Boston Towne to its beans.

May I add that we concur in the humble opinion that getting home was the best feature of an excellent day.

1959
The Missing Fork

I t's the little things that count, and if somebody will just tell
me where I can catch a three-tined kitchen fork, about so
big and so long, things may improve about the old homestead.
We've lost ours.

You would expect if the roof blew off the manor, or the foundation settled under the parlor, some degree of consternation
would set in, but the simple loss of a three-tined kitchen fork
might be borne up under with some fortitude. This is not so, for
the progress of our domestic program has gone to pot, and
unless I can find a fork soon the future is gloomy and unprom-
ising.

"I've misplaced my little fork," she said, one day, I suppose it
was a month ago. I was meditating on some abstruse hypothesis
at the time, and didn't pay much attention, but a few days later
she said, "I wish I could find my little fork!"

After a few more times I said, "What's with this little fork
stuff?" "Why," she said, "the little one with three prongs, the
one your mother gave me. And it didn't go out with the swill!"

We still say "swill" around here.

Things do go out with it. Every time I clean out a hog pen I
find artifacts long supposed gone forever, and all of the things
a hog has no use for. She said she had gone down and looked.
I did, too, and I also poked around on the compost heap, and

gave the duck pen a scrutiny, throwing the ducks into a tizzy. But the fork could not be found and we had constant moan over the disappearance. Not one bit of housework can be done, right that is, without that fork.

I remember my mother did give it to her. My mother was ever the practical one. It was an antique of sorts, something long in the family somewhere, sort of an old wives' thing. It was approximately the size of an ordinary dinner fork, with a riveted wooden handle, and it had only the three tines. It was steel instead of silver, and the tines had a bit more upward bend to them than an ordinary fork. Made it more grasping.

When we set up housekeeping Mother contributed several smallish items like that, the kind of things wedding guests and the social set wouldn't think of—or give if they did. We had 17 table lamps and 33 pickle dishes, but Mother said, "I couldn't keep house without one of these," and she gave us the fork. It didn't get put on the table with the fancy things—nor did it get put in the barn after the ceremony.

It was a "utility" fork, of course. It would spear the brisket right out of the boiled-dinner kettle, and nothing would turn bacon so well. It could flip rolls out of the tins, stir scrambling eggs, and filch an olive right out of the bottle.

So, we exhausted the chances, and still didn't find it. It must be gone. Every time I go into the kitchen I hear the lamentations. Everything is harder without it, so much more clumsy. "Look how I have to chase doughnuts around!" she says, and it's true—the little fork always snagged them so pertly.

We went looking for another. I took her to the city, and while I attended to my philanthropies she went up one side and down the other and asked in all the stores for a three-tined fork. None of them had one. None of them had anything even like it, she said, but in one store she bought a two-tined fork because the man was so nice. It is heavier and bigger than the favorite, and she hoped it might do—but it doesn't. No character.

Then one day I had a chance, so I made the rounds of the

stores she missed, and I saw about every kind of fork currently available. They run heavily to a three-tined picnic fork with an extension shank on them, so you can thread on a hot dog and cook it over a fire six feet away. That's no kind of a fire to cook a hot dog on, anyway.

I became alarmed at the situation among our storekeepers— they would hear me ask for a small three-tined kitchen fork (holding my hands about so) and they would beam and come trotting back with one of these barbecue spits with the long handle. It proves they are disposed to trade and friendly, but I can't say it is evidence of deep powers of comprehension. I looked at about fifteen of these forks, and couldn't fight it any longer. I went home.

It is just a little three-tined steel fork with a wooden handle, about like a dinner fork—and two tines are no good and four tines are no good. You must take my word for it, I don't know why. It may be feminine logic, a phase of philosophy in which I am interested but not well versed. Anyway, that's what it is, and I'd like to buy one. Just one.

"Maybe," she said. "Maybe if you write a piece about it somebody will know." She seldom, if ever, thus presumes on my extracurricular literary pursuits, and this shows how serious it is. If it works, I may get some scrambled eggs again without lumps.

I'd say, offhand, the monetary value shouldn't exceed a dollar at the utmost, even with today's expanded ideas. But when a family's entire happiness and future security is at stake, price is no object.

All Forks Lead to the Gould Farm

A small sampling of the flood of letters (with forks or offers thereof) received by the Goulds from warmhearted and appreciative readers. John, momentarily speechless at such generous response to his plea, will respond later.

Restoring Happiness

Dear Mr. Gould:

I have thoroughly enjoyed your articles in the *Christian Science Monitor*, but none ever struck such a sympathetic chord as the one about the missing fork. Mrs. Gould has my most profound sympathy, and you also because you suffer, too, when your scrambled eggs are lumpy and the doughnuts get too brown while she is struggling to retrieve them out of the hot fat with a four-tined fork that is too wide to insert into the holes and too blunt to harpoon them with. I know, because I am a three-tined, wooden-handled table-fork enthusiast, too.

Now this letter isn't being written just for the sake of prattle. The object of it is to restore happiness in your home once more by offering you one of my three-tined, wooden-handled forks. I am the proud possessor of half a dozen of them of three vintages, one dating back probably to the time that my mother started housekeeping, 68 years ago.

In my opinion, a three-tined, wooden-handled fork is like a garden hoe in that it hasn't reached its peak of efficiency until it has had considerable use; and I'm sure the brisket of beef would respond much more readily to a jab with a secondhand one.

ORA M. STAEDELI

PEORIA ILL

84

In Appreciation

Dear Mr. and Mrs. Gould:

If you don't receive at least a hundred letters and two dozen three-tined forks in the mail I'll be awfully surprised. We have one, and I will be happy to ship it to you.

The reason I didn't send it the minute I finished reading your delightful piece was the certain knowledge that you might be oversupplied since everyone else, even as I, would feel that a three-tined kitchen fork is little enough gratuity for the many hours of delightful reading provided by the Gould family and farm.

My fork measures 6¾" from tip to tine-end. It was given to me by my maternal grandmother who said they used it as a table fork when she was a young girl. They were rather poor, her father being a Methodist minister (I suspect he really was a circuit rider) who housed his family in a sod house on the Kansas plain. It (the fork) has a black wooden handle and the steel is not stainless, needing frequent applications of elbow grease and Brillo to keep it shining.

Medina, Wash. Jo Ann D. Patterson

Answer to an S.O.S.

Dear Mrs. Gould:

I know just how you feel! I have a knife that I call "Grammie" because it was given to me when I was about nine years old by a woman in her 80's—and I am no spring chicken! Originally it was the size of a regular case knife, but it has seen so much wear that it is now only about four inches long and tapers off at the end to almost a peak. When I lose track of "Grammie" I send out an S.O.S.

The three-tined fork that I sent you yesterday has seen better days but I figured your versatile husband could pry the prongs apart and straighten it up a bit.

I'll bet you have a woodshed full of three-tined forks by now!
Concord, N.H.   ELEANOR DARRAH

A Traveled Fork

Dear John:

Your lament in the *Monitor* of March 26 touched me deeply. Never let it be intimated that the native-born do not rush to each other's assistance. I searched and found one.

Coming to you is a 3-tiner fork. Steel prongs with sharp points. Steel handle with wood grips riveted on. One piece steel, so you can bend it to any angle you desire.

This is a traveled fork. Starting in Kinsman, Ohio, it went to Decorah, Iowa, in 1859. Thence to Albert Lea, Minnesota, and then back to Kinsman. Then to Cleveland, then East Orange, back in 1896, to Washington, D.C., for six years after 1918, then back to East Orange. Then it went along on a trip from Boston to Seattle, down the coast, back and forth over the desert, back through Texas to New Jersey. Then up to Alaska in 1953, riding the Alcan. It speared fried fish on the banks of the Yukon above Whitehorse. Did not turn up any gold. Back to East Orange.

Now I would like for you to give it a home if it pleases Gould & Co. Nobody left around here to use it in any manner to which it is accustomed. This fork likes to be in action. May your family be able to skillet it for the years to come.

East Orange, N.J.   EDWARD W. COFFIN

For the Pink-Aproned Lady

Dear John Gould:

Can appreciate exactly how the little lady of pink and yellow aprons in your life feels being without a three-tined, black-handled fork. I'd be simply lost too! So am sending her one of the old set we've had since I can remember. When we were young-sters 'twas our "everyday" flatware. Since its retirement to the basement we've never been without one or two to use for every-thing under the sun—just can't turn meat or bacon without a three-tined fork.

One by one they've found their way into friends' and rela-tives' kitchens and they feel the same way we do—"just can't cook without them." We have enjoyed your "Dispatch from the Farm" as long as you've been contributing it. You've given us so many hours of pleasure down through the years. Do hope this fork is just what Mrs. Gould wants and now you can have your scrambled eggs, etc., again.   MARGUERITE GRANGER

INDIANAPOLIS IND

To the Rescue

Dear Mr. Gould:

Once more—"It's a long way from California to Maine," and a number of three-tined forks nearer to you may have come to the rescue before this reaches you. If not, there is one here that I will so happily send for the sake of the little lady, the bacon and scrambled eggs, etc., and you, Mr. Gould, whose many articles I've read and enjoyed in the *Monitor*. So, if and when I hear from you that this is the "one" you need, it will be mailed promptly.

Berkeley, Calif.   HELEN DUNN

From a Sister 'Maineac'

Dear Mr. Gould:

Cheer up! The three-tiners may be scarce but they're not extinct! And here's one to prove it. So it will be smooth scram-bled eggs and nice round-holed doughnuts for you once again—and wouldn't I love to be right there when they are served! For you see I know all about those specialties—I'm a "Maineac"!

I really have roots in Maine in spite of having lived in Chicago since the early 1880's!

From its first issue in 1908 The Christian Science Monitor has been in our home continuously; and I wish I could tell you how much the Farm Dispatches have meant to this Westerner with Maine roots!

The enclosed three-tined fork was one of the very few things I brought here with me! Father's sister had given it to me in York many years ago and it was old at that time! And if you hadn't written I would never have known of your disastrous plight. I'm tickled pink to be able to help restore order in the Gould house—unless someone else beats me to it, for you may have a regular avalanche of three-tined forks! It wouldn't surprise me!

Chicago, Ill.   MARION L. BRAGDON

1959
The Pink Ap'n Is A-Sing

For some weeks I've wondered how to commence this report, and I suppose the best way is to stop wondering and begin. It has to do with three-tined forks, and if anybody was ever thrust into orbit by his own firecracker, 'twas I.

May I underline, first of all, that there really was a three-tined steel kitchen fork; that my helpmeet did lose it; that she did say she couldn't keep house without it; and that she did beseech me to inquire in the public print where one might apply to get another. Thus a "Dispatch" on the subject appeared, and we hadn't the vaguest notion of what we were starting.

The truth is that there has not been such a spate of response since your editor and I first cooked up the idea of these Dispatches—and to me this is a puzzling thing. Of all the variant topics we've touched on, pertaining generally to human affairs, the last I'd have picked for an all-out winner would be the three-tined fork.

And it is embarrassing that there are so many of you, but only one of me. When the forks came by dozens and the letters by scores, there were a couple of days of amazement, and then the throwing of hands in the air. To all joining in the collective planning, preparation, making and distributing of a great family journal, such response is a joy. You don't always realize how far the candle beams, until one day some such item clicks. But I'm stumped at finding a way to acknowledge adequately such an outpouring.

Even as I contemplated the task, Daylight Saving came in, and I lost an hour. Then President Eisenhower proposed upping the letter stamp to a nickel, which seemed a personal affront! And the mail showed no sign of letting up, or the forks of ceasing to come. Indeed, before the first letters could be opened, noted, and appreciated, there already had arrived one from a gentleman who said he had sent a fork, and as I hadn't acknowledged it, perhaps it had been lost and he should put a tracer on it! (I wrote him at once, of course.)

There aren't many places we haven't heard from—Boston, the Middle West, the South, the Pacific Coast, Canada, England (a couple of forks received from here were over 300 years old). There has even been time to hear from Australia.

But quite apart from the editorial satisfaction that comes from finding such a plural topic, my "pink ap'n" is a-sing in the kitchen, a fork in each hand and another Carmen-like atwixt her teeth, and she is as happy as a clam at high tide, as gay as a banana split, and no task is too arduous. She can flip doughnuts again, get pickles from the brine, and the scrambled eggs are smooth as a smelt.

There were two-three ladies wrote in and said goodness, they'd lost their forks, too, and if perchance we got an oversup-

ply, would we share? We shore, sending to each the name of
the original donor so thank-you's could be made.

She thinks I should shape up some pine boards, long panels
to go above the cupboards in the kitchen, where she can attach
the forks in a permanent exhibit. She has each laid out with
a tag on it, telling who sent it. However, Postmaster General
Summerfield was careless, and a few packages came through
rimwracked beyond identification. There were also several
anonymous arrivals. Some came with ribbons tied on; many had
notes giving family histories.

Although all were essentially the same kind of fork, and satisfied the definitions, there were many styles. Some had bone
handles, some ivory, some wood—and a few had homemade
handles showing ancient repair. Most showed long years of use,
but a few were brand new—indicating they may still be had in
stores if you know where to look. And also, as I said, that
money is no object when the lady of the house is in want.

Besides all the forks that came, dozens of letters said, "If you
don't receive one, let me know and I have one I'll send." The
essence of the whole experience, perhaps, is found in the pre-
dominance of letters which recalled such forks in the hands of
grandmothers, aunts, smoothly doing household chores—
happy memories hitherto neglected. Some of these letters
showed a refrain . . . wonder whatever became of that fork?

So, it is gratifying to have touched on a subject which pleased
so many, and sparked so many to a tangible response. But that
is "shop talk," and relatively unimportant. The important thing
is the friendliness, neighborliness, kindness and concern. It is
as if we had a fraternity, with the tines standing for abstractions
in triple array.

The whole thing has left us deeply touched and humble, and
feeling very rich amongst a broad membership. When the panels are in place, and the fork "collection" becomes a dominant
theme in our kitchen (the room we live in!) it should be pretty
hard to convince us that an individual is ever an island. If Excali-
bur and Durandal and things like that have become legendary

symbols of morality, how much more potent to us will be the esoteric values of the three-tined fork!

Possibly we can, sooner or later, send off our individual thanks. Certainly we plan to! Meantime, because we thought you'd like to know, we have insinuated this Dispatch. We certainly hope everybody is as happy as we are!

1960
Bana's Back Hall

The lad found himself a job for the summer up in the woods, which I think is a good thing, and he asked me to drive him in. You always go into the woods, and come out. You can spot the casual acquaintance by this — he will say he is going "in to town." But you don't. You go out to town. Then you come back in again. This rides on a special, somewhat selfish, conception all true woodsmen have: That everything important is right there, and the world is remote. This is entirely contrary to the reverse, of course.

Anyway, we threw his gear in the conveyance and in three hours we were approaching the vacation resort where he will preside for the "season."

In the Maine woods, from old logging days down, certain traditions prevail, and certain old terms are kept. For instance, the "dingle." The dingle is a shed, often open-sided, adjoining the cook camp. And an important term is the "back hall." The back hall is the dining and lounging room for the help, and it is a sacred precinct jealously guarded against encroachment by "sports."

People may come as guests to the resort, ready to spend any

amount of money to enjoy the pleasures of lakeside and pine scented proximity—but no fortune can buy the privilege of eating in the back hall. The greasy mechanic who comes in to repair a water pump can eat there. So can the game warden or a telephone lineman. Even a passing timberjack, maybe an alien sneaking the border and shortly to be picked up for illegal entry, can eat there if he chances by on purpose at mealtime—but Wall Street money isn't green enough to buy a seat.

The rule isn't unbreakable, of course. Occasionally a family will want to start a hike early, and instead of waiting for the guests' dining room to open they will be fed in the back hall. All summer long, after that, they'll brag about it. "We ate in the back hall!" they'll say. But they had to be invited, first.

We arrived about three in the afternoon, and while the lad was stowing his gear in the cabin he'll use this summer, I sat in the back hall and talked to Bana. Bana is a great-grandmother, and has been woodswise since she was a tot. She traveled the north country, even up beyond the St. Lawrence, when she was a youngster, and says, "I was too young to remember some of it."

She has cooked and chored in lumber and sporting camps ever since, and naturally many people meet her and think she's fairly local. But if you draw her out you'll find she can talk about Bombay and Cape Town and many another place she's been off and on. Bana wouldn't be fazed a bit if she got appointed to the Supreme Court tomorrow—she'd just pack up and go, and do a good job. Neither does it faze her to cook for a back hall, which is what she was doing then.

At three o'clock, nobody much was around. There was a man fixing planks on the wharf and a fellow painting canoes, and two women putting linen in the cabins. The kitchen staff was due, and the waitresses were expected. The roster hadn't assembled, but the place would open for guests in two days, and at three o'clock there was no way of knowing how many would show for supper. I think housewives will want to ponder on this. Bana had been explaining how Napoleon Comeau used to launch a boat on the surge tide, and she got up from her rocking chair and said, "Well, I might's well start supper."

A back hall, or at least this one, is a log building completely circled with wooden clothespins driven into bit-holes—so everybody will have room to hang clothes, wet or dry, heavy or light. Over the stove are wires for drying mittens and socks. The stove is a Kineo, at least a century old, and up on birch blocks because the stovepipe was too short. This model was made in a Bangor foundry since long-gone, and is noted for the oven doors on each side. It's a bilateral stove, and such a good heater that the legend persists that you could pass a pan of biscuits through from side to side and they would be browned. It burns wood, and has a wide hearth.

Bana began. No hurry, she continued the conversation as she went. She reached down dishes and finished setting the table. Back hall etiquette is traditional—all plates get turned bottom-up, with a cup and saucer on top. Hardware means a knife and fork with the dishes athwart, but the spoons are in a spoon-dish, to be reached for. Salts and peppers, sugar, molasses and syrup, mustard, and such things are at intervals. All food will be in platters and bowls, each to serve himself. And at the end of the meal everybody picks up his own dishes and carries them to the sink.

Bana had a ham baking, and began on the vegetables. She got the potatoes ready, and the green beans and peas. She had a gravy. She opened cans of pears for dessert. And all the time, as the clock wore on, Bana got news of new arrivals. People were coming. Each time, she'd turn toward the long trestle-table and count off places. Mentally, she was keeping track. But it was nearly five before the count went to 20, and it was 32 when supper was ready.

Bana's last contribution was hot sal'ratus biscuits, piping from the oven, acre upon beautiful acre. When she placed a platter of them on the table, you'd see a great waving of hands, and then she'd remove the platter to fill it again.

"Got enough for me?" I asked, and Bana said. "There's always enough." "You know," I said, "the Waldorf-Astoria wouldn't know how to do that!" "No, I s'pose not," said Bana. Then she said, "I was there once, though, and they feed pretty good." I think, coming from Bana's back hall, the big hotel never had a nicer compliment.

1961
A Queen and Biscuits

The Commissioner of Agriculture of the State of Maine, E. L. (Dick) Newdick, recently attended a supper served in the basement of a small-town Maine church, and during the course of the merriment somebody asked him if he didn't think the biscuits were pretty good. Commissioner Newdick thereupon made a fine statement which has not been accorded the general notoriety it deserves. He said, "Well, the five I had were good."

Mrs. Newdick, seated beside him, next made an observation which is equally momentous, for she said, "You had six!"

Now, a vast and irrefutable moral is about to be inculcated, so a more specific description of the circumstances should be afforded. Once a year the Maine Blueberry Industry gathers its forces at Union Fair, held in the town of Union, and holds a promotional program known as the Annual Maine Wild Blueberry Festival. Many pleasant moments prevail, and in the evening the "Maine Blueberry Queen" is selected.

This year she is Miss Monalee Smith of the blueberry town of Brooksville, and if you think hers is a minor distinction in the general perspective, you should have seen the 12 girls she beat. The Miss America pageant, by comparison, is a veritable chamber of horrors, for the blueberry barrens of Maine are certainly not a single-product area. Anyway, after an exhausting afternoon program the several contestants, judges, committee, and visiting dignitaries are whisked from the crowd at the fair and taken to the quiet dining room under the church for a dinner. Mr. Newdick, on route to this repast in the feebleness of hunger, was heard to philosophize: "In Union, there is strength!" The dinner was certainly memorable, and much was made of the biscuits.

Now these biscuits were created by a petite matron of Union whose name is Jackie Hawes. Volunteering to assist in the publication of this supper, she rightly divided the work so the biscuits fell to her, and while another husked the sweet corn and another rolled the pies (Maine wild blueberry pies) she splashed flour around on a breadboard and came up with an acre and a half of real down-Maine baking powder biscuits which, however stalwart they appeared on the platters, failed to survive the engagement. They were hot, so the application of butter imbued them friendly-like, and created what the trade calls a desire.

To show you, sort-of, it is a recorded fact that Miss Smith, feeling she should not over-indulge before the judging was completed, slyly inserted a couple of these biscuits in her purse, properly wrapped in a paper napkin, and began eating them as soon as the coronation exercises were over. Commissioner Newdick, upon hearing this, wistfully said, "why didn't I think of that?"

Mrs. Newdick, paying the highest compliment one Maine woman can give another, afterward asked Mrs. Hawes for her receet, and notes were taken by your correspondent during the colloquy.

Said Jackie, "I don't have any receet, I just make them." Now, all great and good cooks should notice that, for Jackie adjusts her biscuit quantity automatically to the number of people she is going to serve. She sizes up the company, and then governs herself accordingly. Mrs. Newdick then asked how Jackie had made the particular batch of biscuits with which she had adorned the repast on this occasion, and when stated this way the problem was one Jackie could quickly answer.

The following is a quotation:

"I think it was six cups of flour I used—but I don't use a measuring cup. I just take a tea-cup out of the cupboard and dip. No, I don't sift it. Then I kind of guess how many cups I've used, and put in two teaspoons of baking powder for each cup. Somewhere near. That would be, two-times-six—12 teaspoons, wouldn't it? So, now let's see—some salt. I guess a tablespoon. You know, you just put in some salt, but I'd say about a tablespoon. Next you have to have shortening, and you want two good gobs of it, a couple about the size of an egg—just what it needs. (Business of holding up both hands with the fingers indicating two medium-large hen's eggs.) And then I take a pastry cutter, one of those things you mix shortening into flour with, and if I don't have one handy I use my fingers, and I get it feeling just right before I put in the milk. How much milk? Oh, perhaps a quart. About a quart, I'd say. Then when it feels about right, I take it on the board and knead it some—not too much—and cut the biscuits and put them in the pans. Then I shove them in a 450-oven and take them out when they're done. I guess that isn't very much of a receet, but that's the way I make biscuits."

Commissioner Newdick, being informed that his wife had now acquired the Hawes' recipe for baking-powder biscuits, looked as if he had just heard that all farm commodities had gone up a dollar a bushel, an expression much like one who has found five dollars he didn't know was in the pockets of his old pants, and he rapped on the table with a salt shaker to gain attention, and addressed the candidates for the blueberry queen title somewhat as follows:

"Girls—you are all young and pretty, and a great credit to the state. Many and various honors will come upon you as you course the highway of life, and one of you is to be honored this evening with a coveted title. But I hope all of you will learn to bake good biscuits."

1962
That One-Time Simplicity

Y ou know," I said, looking up from the vast bookkeeping connected with my many philanthropies, "It's been a long time since we've had a mess of dried beef on potatoes." Truth is, it has. Used to be almost a staple in the old days—made a good, hearty meal that everybody dove into, and all at once it came to me that it's been a long time.

"Well," she welled, "I was going to give you a three-way choice for supper tonight—hummingbird tongues on Melba toast with Turkish Delight, Mongolian pheasant under glass with kumquat soufflé, and dried beef on potatoes with hardtack."

"I would take the dried beef," I said, and she said, "It's the most expensive."

This turns out to be disturbingly so. What, from the memories of youth, was always a great way to stretch short pennies into the greatest good for the greatest number has become an epicure's ne plus ultra of the age of enlightenment, and she has been hanging back on dried beef so she might have more money to spend for food.

When I hear somebody ask, "What is the world coming to?" I always make answer that I do not know.

She observes, too, that when she does buy some dried beef these days it is not the same as it used to be. It used to come in fairly large slices, rolled together adroitly so it would fill the bottle or can. Now it is otherwise; you get two-three sheets wrapped around a gorm of shreds and crumbs, and pride of workmanship is gone. The bundle doesn't open out into the same product.

It has variously been observed by astute observers that a great many of the good things to eat that adorned the simple life back on the farm were cheap. This fact was known to the custodian of the family exchequer, but was not suspected by the others. We thought we ate those things because they were the best things in the world to eat. Take baked beans. On a farm that regularly laid out 10 to 15 acres of baking beans there wasn't anything any cheaper. But when adorned with honest pork, laced with dark molasses, and suitably infused with love and ginger, a pot of beans on the supper table was about as high off the hog as anybody wanted. We thought that was pretty good.

In the days when hands were busy all day at outdoor work and exercise was a process of life an appetite was a presumption of ingestion. And if you figured it cost maybe a quarter of a cent a portion to set baked beans before a family, you figured it high because there were always some left over for breakfast. And you were serving something the Waldorf chefs couldn't match, and can't. Put a pan of buttermilk biscuits alongside, some crisp, juicy sour pickles, and an apple pie, and if you listened you could hear mighty Zeus on high Olympus whimpering in envy as he toyed with his plain old nectar and ambrosia. This is true, because I was there.

Dried beef didn't cost much. It was supposed to be some kind of an orphan of the packing industry, and although it had a Chicago by-line on it we understood it was really South American meat and a by-product. For a few cents Mother could get a big jar of the stuff, and with the magic of her kitchen wand could translate it magnificently.

If she wanted to raise supper into the million-dollar category, she could bake the potatoes, but usually she just boiled them. Understand that we had potatoes pushing up against the floor timbers down cellar and the cows and pigs helped us eat them, so 10 or 15 bushels one way or the other worried nobody. So there was a big iron pot for boiling potatoes, and it never cooled off. People today don't use potatoes the way we did. We put them in bread, and made soup of them—not the cold, clammy stuff with the fancy name, but real hot soup. We had fried potatoes for breakfast, even, and with a bacon fat flavor they're hard to beat. And for dried beef the boiled hot potato was just the checker.

It got smashed on the plate, with a gob of butter on top, and then we dipped into the bowl to cover it with creamed dried beef. The top-notch kind would have a half-dozen hard-boiled eggs worked into the sauce, and the little chunks of yolk would look up and grin at you like a burst of sunshine. Everything was fine and dandy. The dried beef had a smoky, salty flavor that suggested the exotic; giving you a Westphalian ham or Labrador gasperaux effect.

Everybody got up full as ticks, replete and surfeited, convinced this was the best of all possible worlds and that fortune had favored us with the greatest cook ever to grasp a spoon.

Well, she argues that when she goes to the store to spend $25 for a little bag of modern goodies to stave off starvation, and her thoughts turn to dried beef, prudence suggests there are better ways to spend the last digits in the budget. As an occasional experience with the expensive, yes; but the one-time simplicity of dried beef and boiled potatoes has been priced out of sight in the great progress of logistics. "If we were millionaires," she says, "We could have it every meal," and I can't think of a better reason to be a millionaire.

1963
Sent by Mail

Inasmuch as I seem to write you folks a letter every week, I'm interested that the Post Office Department has decreed the official size of automated mail, and how long, O Cataline, must we endure these unbridled audacities? What size and shape should a letter be? Must composition, so elusive and demanding, now fit through the slot of a machine? What news doth yonder courier bring, and what are its dimensions? One day a man received a letter and he tore it open eagerly and read: "Is the weather with you as rude and boisterous as it is with us? All here is tempest and inundation. . . ."

What size and shape were Pliny's letters?

One of the most notable epistles in State of Maine history is recorded by Holman Day, who tells how a fish dealer in Portland brought comfort to his displaced daughter in Denver, Colorado:

> . . . he went to a ten-cord pile of cod
> and he pulled the biggest out,
> A jib-shaped crittur, broad's a sail,
> —three feet from tail to snout.
> And he pasted a sheet of postage
> stamps from snout clear down
> to tail,
> Put on a quick-delivery stamp, and
> sent the cod by mail.

Here was a letter of unique fragrance and import—but it could not be handled today by transistors. A codfish is the wrong size and shape for the swift completion of appointed rounds.

This is a shame. When Grandfather's estate was being settled and I bid on the old farm at the auction called for by the administrator, I took down the pine-board sign by the road that said, "For Sale," wrote on the address of my betrothed, and mailed it to her to prove that we'd have a place to live some day. Postal clerks must have paused to peruse it as it went along, and I hope they suspicioned some of the deep sentiment it conveyed. The scantling was delivered promptly, as first-class mail, and within the hour she was planning the curtains for the kitchen windows.

When two people apart require the services of a postman to bring their thoughts together, it is not always likely the precise measurements can be wisely foretold. "When I read your letter," a gentleman once wrote, "I am comforted as if by your amiable presence; but once I am finished solace waits upon the next."

This, translated into modernese, would run, no doubt, like this: "Your six-and-a-half by three-and-five-eighths at hand, etc. . . . "

Will Grant up at Kennebago Lake once received a memorable letter from a gentleman in California who, the previous summer, had been at Kennebago and was disturbed by the way porcupines chewed at the buildings. He wrote a 36-page letter, longhand on both sides of the paper, with some suggestions about restraining the beasts, and signed it, "Yours in haste." Will kept the letter always and used to show it to people, and its dimensions were tremendous in every direction. What size should a letter be?

But Blaise Pascal once apologized because his letter was so long—he didn't have time, he said, to make it shorter. But shortness isn't always a virtue—the beloved Professor Carberry at Brown University is on record with a short note that said, "Isn't that terrible what happened to Charles?"

The many-sided Lewis Carroll once wrote "Eight or Nine

Wise Words about Letter Writing," and some of it is helpful. Address the envelope first, he says, for otherwise you may write right up to post time, and then have too little time to do a legible job, or you may find you don't have a stamp in the house. If, he says, you write, "Enclosed find so-and-so . . ." then by all means go and get whatever it is and put it in the envelope at once. He seems to think a letter which says, "Enclosed find five pounds" ought to have five pounds in it. Yet what if you have already stamped and addressed a five-by-seven envelope, and you decide to enclose something seven-by-nine? He doesn't say.

He spends some thought on closing lines, which is important, and he once closed a letter by writing, "Please say to so-and-so for me anything you think would be most likely to surprise her. . . ." Don't you relish the thoughts of the Postmaster General passing on the size and shape of such things? Bill Nye, made postmaster in Laramie, wrote to thank the Postmaster General and offer his cooperation, and he started the letter, "My dear General . . ." Mr. Nye's letter will be found in numerous anthologies, regardless of shape and size. It might never have been written, however, if Mr. Nye, unequipped with acceptable length, breadth and thickness, had been obliged to delay while he walked across town to get some approved stationery. Think on this, I beg of you.

I once had a fine letter from a gentleman who wrote on the opened-up side of a paper bag. He wrote, "Dear sir—I don't owe you no money and I ain't going to pay you none, so stop sending me bills." I found he was right, and didn't send him no more, and he never did. So as a letter, it served, and must have been the right size and shape.

1964
Molasses and Oatmeal

A most amazing thing has just come to my attention. The president of the Quaker Oats Company has admitted that he never heard of anointing his product with molasses. Indeed, he has confided that the idea is so wonderful that he will now direct his nutritionists to set up a "discovery" meeting, when they will hold their hands in the air ecstatically and declare that molasses is good on oatmeal.

Close followers of my rural wisdom will know this is an ancient theme. In my tantrums against profane change, I have lamented not only the drop-off in quality of both molasses and oat cereals, but have railed against the softening of our public resistance to mediocrity.

It will hardly be a return to basics if the president of Quaker Oats now "discovers" that saponified, ultracentrifugated, chemically-bleached molasses goes well with quick-cooking and instantized rolled oats. Yet, we all know there will be no great public objection to this false gallop of semantics, and that a whole fad may well be generated by the announcements. I even expect that some day soon somebody will "discover" soap.

I am going to hold in reserve the magnificent news that maple sirup, also, goes well with oats, and I will spring it on the industry only after I see how they make out with molasses. To me, right now, the highest evidence of the decline of our perceptions in this whole area is the television commercial where a cane sirup faintly fused with maple flavor is advertised by showing a sap bucket hanging on a pine tree.

And this isn't away out, either, for just this week our Maine Department of Agriculture released a publicity picture in which "Miss Maple Queen of 1964" is shown boring a tap-hole in a swamp maple. I suggested to the man that it might be better to use a sugar maple, and he said, "Aw, nobody will know the difference."

Isn't that, dear and trusted readers, the answer to all this?

I would like, if it might be done, to sit the president of Quaker Oats at a certain table that rises up in my mind's eye, where breakfast is about to be served. A slanting bar of the rising sun's solid gold comes in at the six-over-eight east window and illuminates the articles on the table. There is a heavy crockery jug adorned with thistles and holding rich, sweet, Jersey cream.

Another jug, equally sturdy, contains thick Barbados molasses. Then there is an ancient sugar bowl whose top was broken long ago, in which the silverware is stashed, handles up. Another sugar bowl, with a cover, contains sugar. Next is the caster with its oil, vinegar, mustard, pepper and salt. An assortment of jellies and jams, and pickle relishes. And over this centerpiece, directly in the glint of the sun, there is a spread of cheesecloth to keep off the houseflies.

Now, there are no houseflies in my grandmother's kitchen, but tradition called for this spread of cloth, and if Grandmother were still keeping house she would still have a cheesecloth. My grandfather is already seated at the head of the table, and you may see my grandmother behind him, at the black and nickel stove, dishing a soup plate of oatmeal from an iron pot that certainly wasn't bought yesterday. You will observe, if you are the president of Quaker Oats, that an attitude of expectancy characterizes Grandfather. He has already finished the barn chores, silenced the squealing swine, and turned the crank on the Westfalian separator.

About the time Grandmother turns from the stove with the steaming dish of oat meal (not rolled oats) my grandfather will pick up one edge of the cheesecloth and prepare for her arrival. He will take a dessert spoon, and then reach out the jugs of cream and molasses. He will fill a cup with cream and another cup with molasses, and then return the jugs under the cloth. When Grandmother sets the dish down, he is ready.

The president of Quaker Oats will now see my grandfather dip a spoon of his porridge, douse it in the cup of molasses, lave it in the cup of cream, and then with the fingers of his left hand part the vistas and dells of his wide-white beard and insert the sustenance into the originating alimentary orifice. The president of Quaker Oats would then see what we children vastly admired—the pleased expression that came into the old man's pale blue eyes, and the magnificent activity of the whiskers on his neck when he swallowed and his Adam's Apple gave assent.

This old kitchen would certainly be a better place to "discover" molasses and oatmeal than any congregation of modern nutritionists acting on a flat from the front office.

1965
A Premium You Could Write On

O ne of the bread bakers has put a big billboard on the state road, and it gladdens the passing world with the important news that the shortening now being used contains 21 percent less fat. Thus we course the accelerated journey of our wonderful times. This extra bonus of nonfat-fat will make us all want to buy this fine product.

In my youth about the only bonus I can think of that derived from canny purchasing was the little pieces of pasteboard that separated the layers of Shredded Wheat. These were handy for many things, and none went to waste. Oh, don't let this sound like a gratuitous endorsement of shredded wheat biscuits, which I never particularly liked. What I'm endorsing is the basic marketing principles of Shredded Wheat, who simply sold shredded wheats, and didn't urge us to buy them because we got paper to do school work on. Those wonderful little sheets of cardboard were never figured into the deal.

I'm back in the days of cooked cereals, naturally. We usually had oatmeal, laced with molasses and tied down with pan cream, and it was cooked all night in a double-boiler, which was an implement of homemaking now almost forgotten. Now and then, to spice up the outlook, the oatmeal shifted to cornmeal mush, and maybe to a wheat cereal. Whichever it was, it got dipped by a long-handled spoon into a soup plate, and if we didn't eat it we wouldn't get any fried potatoes, eggs and meat, biscuits and pie.

But there were already several dry cereals on the market, which were considered all right for summertime, when a person could eat light. We children considered it a treat to tackle, occasionally, the novelty of puffed wheats, shredded wheats, and corn flakes. And I always had a preference for shredded wheats because of the sheets of paper. I am happy to report there has been no great change, for to document this splendid report I went to the store and bought the first package of shredded wheat biscuits we've had in the house in 40 years, and the separating stationery is still to be had. It was truly a wonderful thing, to find in this maelstrom of change, that one smallish matter has been faithful. I feel this strongly overcomes the normal editorial reluctance to give free publicity to a commercial venture.

Paper wasn't too easy to come by back in those times. We were always frugal with what we had, and did our sums small so we'd have room. Mother used to keep a shredded wheat card behind the mirror in the kitchen, for her egg records. I remember Father used a whole sheet one time to send a note to Mort Guptill, saying, "Will you come Sat. and help me with the well," and Mother chided him first for using a whole sheet for such a short message, and then for writing a note at all because Mort couldn't read anyway. Word of mouth would have been good enough, and the shredded wheats would have lasted that much longer.

Shredded Wheat paper was negotiable. A man came one evening and wanted to borrow money from my uncle to buy a mowing machine, and Uncle wrote out a note on a shredded wheat slip. Later, my uncle needed the money, so he discounted the note at the bank. Somehow this implies an integrity that comforts me as I contemplate in later times the new kind of bread that has 21 percent less fat in the fat.

I can aver, too, that shredded wheats had value over and beyond the homework we did on them. They made an authoress of my mother, for one thing. Mother never wrote much of anything except notes to my teachers, but the clean shape of the shredded wheat teased her into excellence, and she composed notes that deserve historical attention. At first she used to write, "Please excuse John for being late, he was delayed." But these ripened into masterpieces of composition: "Honored and esteemed sir—In the vast press of matutinal obligations, coupled with the reluctance of a water pump to thaw out by reasonable persuasion, time elapsed until my son fell upon a deficit schedule. Please be so good as to make allowances, etc."

Well, my father had an odd business that kept him away from home a week at a time, and then he would be home for a week, and while he was away the barn chores were all mine. I would hear the school bell ringing demandingly across the fields, and while my mates were gathering for opening exercises I would still be coaxing a calf to drink, or trying to get the hay thrown down. Mother would have a note ready by my dinner bucket if one were needed, and I would come charging into school and hand it to the principal.

It was on a shredded wheat that my mother wrote the greatest note-to-a-teacher of all times. She had patiently explained to the gentleman that family circumstances obliged me to stick to the last, and that while she regretted my frequent tardiness, she was doing the best she could and his understanding would be appreciated. My father, also, had put in a word of explanation. But the principal still thought he was obliged to pursue the matter, and one day he gave me a note to take home to Mother which said, "Isn't there something we can do to get John to school on time?"

Mother used a whole shredded wheat. She wrote back, "Don't start until he gets there."

1966
Haunts of Culture

M r. Dornbusch, the city feller, came again for our annual wilderness outing, and by courtesy of the Great Northern Paper Company we rusticated 10 miles of raspberries beyond the ne-plus-nobody of Scott Brook, where Mr. Del Bates is bull of the cock shop.Mr. Bates is one of the best lumber camp ink slingers and wangan custodians in the business, and is a pivot point betwixt the distant directors of the corporation and the gyppos, shantyboys and pushers of the route.

I'm sure the vocabulary of the Maine woods will puzzle many, and your civilized dictionaries will be little help. Del Bates runs the office and company store and does the bookkeeping for a major contract-job. Henri Marcoux is the *entrepreneur de bois,* and it is Del's job to keep a company eye on Henri and his crew. Few, except the "super-numeraries," get to tour such a wild, backwoods region while a cutting is going on, but with a sheet of Maine-made paper that said, "This will pass . . ." Bill, the city feller, and I made camp beyond the chain.

The 10 miles of wild raspberries stretch from Scott Brook to

Caucomongomoc Dam, so Bill and I invited Del Bates to come over the next evening and assist us in the monumental delight of a raspberry shortcake that scaled out about two cords and a half. Except for those the bears get, these raspberries usually bud, set, fructify and drop off, so we did not feel we were overdoing a few pailsful. We had barely popped the biscuits into the heat when Mr. Bates arrived, eager for the fray and clearly a hungry man who knew where the answer could be found. The main event was preceded by a beef stew and a sunset, and accompanied by intelligent conversation.

One of the more charming facets of our forest region, remote and often lonely, is the nature and complexion of the people you meet there. Mr. Bates has a home and family in Patten, was at one time a member of the Maine State Legislature, and is the son of a famous "walking boss"—a man who had two or more lumber camps under his command and "walked" from one to the other.

Del said he was a good man, but a hard one, and in a rugged, forthright manner he got the lumber to mill while inculcating the virtues and verities in eight children. With Del, he rightly assessed developing talents, and he sent him to Boston to take a business course at the Bryant & Stratton School. This formal training, added to what Del already knew of scaling, sluicing, toting, yarding, etc., led to a cock shop (camp office) job, and for 16 years Del has presided over the Scott Brook operation. Full of raspberry shortcake, Del lapsed into reminiscence.

"To show you how my father worked (he said) you take Sunday mornings. My mother and us boys took care of the cows and horses and pigs all week, but he'd come out of the woods Saturday, and Sunday morning he'd do the chores. And he would always call just one of us boys to help him.

"Now, what he'd do—he'd call whichever one of us got in last on Saturday night. I don't know how he knew, but he always did. Last one in got rousted out first. I remember once I was unavoidably detained, and it was about three o'clock when I got home, and I took great care to get into bed unannounced. But he knew, and come five o'clock he gave me a poke and told me to get up and help him. It didn't take long to spend that night."

Then Del changed the subject. "The pursuit of culture has always been my strong point. It is not easy to pursue culture in the places I have had at my disposal. But to look at me—old, worn, weary and woodsqueer after a lifetime of cordwood, boiled beans and swamp-companions, you'd never know that Padderooski once played me a private, personal concert."

Del, with good story-telling art, paused to allow full appreciation. Bill, the city feller, leaned forward and said, "Do you mean the pianist, Ignace Jan Paderewski, who was prime minister of Poland and the great champion of independence?"

"I do," said Del. "The very man."

"I don't know how many others achieved this honor," he went on, "but for a little boy from Patten thirsting for the finer things of life, eager, bright-eyed and willing, the Great Padderooski once ran through his 'Minuet in G,' and in memory, even now, amongst the whine of chainsaws and generator, I can still hear the haunting beauty of his exquisite talent." Del paused again.

"Well," he explained. "It was when I was in school in Boston. Padderooski was giving a concert at Symphony Hall, and he had his private railroad car on a siding in Back Bay, and I came along with my books under my arm and he was in there practicing. Everybody else kept walking by, but I stopped and listened for two hours and I never heard anything so pretty before or since."

So, you see, far up beyond the advertised haunts of culture, beyond the chain, through 10 miles of raspberries, we met a man with a precious and unique memory—an adder and subtracter of spruces and firs, for whom Padderooski once played—privately.

1967
Unfinished Business

The State of Maine had a lovely snowstorm to welcome us home from our wanderings in Europe, and we saw nothing over there that was half so pretty. Our children and their mates had a rip-snortin' blaze on the livingroom hearth, and the hot blueberry pie they manufactured for supper tasted good after three months of the strange devices the Europeans eat for dessert. Inside our front door, neatly tied day by day, was the mail that had come.

Before we left home (as I related at the time) I wrote to all the companies and told them we should be away. I mistrust the computer machine, and now I find this mistrust justified. Not one of the companies was able to punch the right key and find me, and all the time we were away the electronic wheels ground inexorably and business went on as usual. I have three months of duns, just as if I hadn't written any letters at all.

And also in the mail is a nice letter from a banker who says I made a lot of work for myself. He says I should have gone to my bank, where they have a special service to handle the affairs of absent clients. They would have answered my mail, paid my bills, and for a reasonable fee all would have been serene on my return.

This is a good thing to know, but I notice that the computer-machine corporations that couldn't adjust to my absence include the bank I would have gone to if I had known about this.

I suppose there are a few items of unfinished business, and then you'll hear no more about our trip. One is: I wrote home about the ease with which we moved from one country to another, through customs and immigration, and suggested this would probably not be true when we tried to reenter the United States. This proved to be so. Our officials are all right, and I have no complaints. They were courteous, kindly and competent. But the regulations they administrate merit scrutiny and repair. We found that foreigners traveling with us were importing all manner of effects, including household furniture, but I was called to account for a jacket I had bought on tour and had worn every day for two months.

There is a perplexing double standard penalizing the natural-born citizen. When we came out of Switzerland, bound for Bremen to board the boat home, we then had everything with us that was to be displayed later at the dock in Brooklyn. It took an hour for the United States official to check and compute it— yet at the border station in Konstanz the German officer merely wished us a pleasant journey after glancing at our passport. So, my prognostication was right, and it took us longest to get into our own country.

Some may argue that it is worth it, but we found it is not necessarily true that home is to be yearned for and that great sighs of relief mount up when the eye gazes again on the ancestral lintel and you find the easy-chair by the fire is still there. We certainly experienced nothing abroad that fomented nostalgia. As one often says, one wouldn't care to live there—but in all honesty we saw many places in rural Germany and France where we could live quite happily.

Thanksgiving Day taught us a subtle distinction in this respect. With us the day has always been an occasion for homecoming, of course, and as we rode around Europe and the big moment approached we had some misgivings about our emotions when we knew it was turkey-time. At home our youngsters were meeting at the farm just as always, and we had caught up with one letter that told us the plum pudding had been made and that they would certainly save a big piece for us in the freezer.

On the Wednesday evening we had put up at a comfortable hotel on the old post-square in Waiblingen, Germany, and during supper there was the usual curiosity about the dining room as to the strangers. Somebody spoke to us, introduced us in turn to somebody else, and as often happened we were soon in the center of an enthusiastic group of German linguists who were practicing their school English on us.

During this I chanced to say that tomorrow would be a big holiday in the United States—Thanksgiving, with a turkey feast. The landlady said she had never seen a dressed turkey, and how did we cook it? I remember we had a big fuss over translating "stuffing." And when we came down to breakfast the next morning there was a little note at our table, inviting us to "schicken and pommes-frites" at one hour p.m., please. We dug out our lah-de-dah clothes and dolled up for this, and came down to be served one of the finest meals we had on the whole trip. It was of course priceless, and the landlady wouldn't let me pay. "Nein!" she said. "Heute ist Dankfest!" Perhaps the incidence of a Yankee Twang, coming out of Waiblingen, occasioned some surprise as we offered our remote and distant grace. At any rate, we certainly didn't wish, on that day, that we were at home in the bosom of our family.

We wished the family could have been with us.

1968
Resident Clerk

I t was 94° F, on the porch of the wangan at the Scott Brook lumbercamp of the GNPCo, and inside we found Mr. Delmont Bates at a total of 126°, which includes his Masonic honors.

Being the resident clerk of the aforesaid paper company, Mr. Bates was occupied with the "first order of business" of all lumbercamp clerks. If you have paid attention, you will recall meeting Mr. Bates before, because annually Mr. William Dornbusch of Rye, N.Y., and I visit Mr. Bates in the course of our vacation, and I have customarily rendered a report.

The excessive heat of mid-July had struck into the north country, too, and the Scott Brook wilderness of Maine was just as hot as Rye, N.Y., and Mr. Dornbusch quickly admitted that he had erred in choosing this week. The "first order of business" of the lumbercamp clerk is basic. Mr. Bates told us that some years back a fine new idea had been thought up in the company offices at Bangor, and he had received the mimeographed sheet which instructed him about it. The idea was all right, but the executive had chosen the wrong words in setting it up. The sheet said, "Please make this your first order of business."

Mr. Bates had done as directed, but then he began to think about it, and he cranked the telephone the correct number of times and got himself connected with Felix Fernald over at Pittston Farm. These forest telephone lines are dandy to talk into, but hearing what comes out is often difficult, so Mr. Bates blatted into his end and Mr. Fernald kept saying, "What?" Eventually, however, the conversation succeeded. Mr. Bates said to Mr. Fernald, "You've been at this woodsclerk business a lot longer than I have, and I'd like to have you tell me what, in your opinion, is the first order of business in a lumbercamp?"

Mr. Fernald didn't hesitate an instant. He said, "The first order of business of any lumbercamp clerk is to get the man standing up to a tree so he can cut it down."

Mr. Bates said, "That's what I thought."

But in the heat wave that accompanied our arrival at Scott Brook the first order of business was having problems. It was just too hot for anything, and production was lagging. "Fait chaud!" was the only topic. We did not sleep under blankets every night, and the trout were so deep in the mud our icthyologic explorations were curtailed. We spent a good part of our time in the lake, as opposed to on it. As a consequence, we had a very clean time. We saw eight deer, one duck, two coots and a sandpiper, and they all had their tongues hanging down.

One afternoon Mr. Dornbusch was agile enough to collect a 12-inch breakfast—a singular collation that in other years has always been in the plural. It was our only catch. Otherwise we spent considerable time in the vicinity of Mr. Bates, who cheated the hot tedium by relating true experiences from his veracious past.

He said that one time in his younger days he ran for the state legislature, and was very proud to proceed to the august halls in Augusta and represent his native Patten. He came down full of wonder, and spent some time meeting people and familiarizing himself with the processes. Everybody was kind to him, and a great deal of honest advice was offered without charge. Then, after a few weeks, the first bills began to come out of committee, and Mr. Bates found that in principle he was opposed to most of them on the grounds that they were expensive. He had been brought up in a poor, but honest, environment, and he was morally opposed to prodigality. He mentioned this to some of his colleagues.

In short, it was soon observed that Mr. Bates was not bending submissively to the party will, and steps were taken to persuade him into more generous channels. One after another his new-found friends approached him and made suggestions about how he should vote. But Mr. Bates was not about to be persuaded, and many a bill was sitting on the table waiting for a pledged majority to appear—an impasse Mr. Bates could help alleviate if he would just change his mind. The session seemed to stand still.

At this point Mr. Bates was told that the governor had asked him to drop in for a friendly chat. When Mr. Bates stepped into the executive office the governor was delighted to see him, wrung his hand in unstinting affection, and made some small talk. Shortly the governor was persuasive about these bills, but he, too, soon found out that Mr. Bates was not to be persuaded.

In the end the governor gave up, and he concluded the interview by saying, "Mr. Bates, there must be a number of good men much smarter than you that the citizens of Patten could have sent down here to Legislature!"

Mr. Bates replied, "Yes, sir—there are. Plenty of them. But I was the only one who had a suit of clothes."

1968
Making It Last

It occurred to me this morning while I was prettying up that my shaving brush is 40 years old. Although it has worn down in faithful service I should get another 60 or 70 years from it. It is not an ordinary brush, and at the same time I am not an ordinary shaver.

I have been known to roam the bushland all week in character, where an unkempt countenance is not likely to alarm the porcupines at all, and if I don't go anywhere I put no demands on my brush. I generally don't go anywhere if I can help it.

I bought the brush in 1928 from Eddie Raymond. I was just matriculated in the college of my choice (tuition was $200 a year and they gave me a whopping scholarship of $55—although they never said what for) and for the first time was away from home and Babe Walsh.

Babe was our home-town barber. So when the time came I went into the business section of the college town until I found a barber pole and I went in and Jud Langen cut my hair. I couldn't remember anybody else except Babe ever doing that, but Jud did a fine job and when he got through I handed him 25 cents.

Jud was something of a personality, and upon this largesse

he struck an attitude, fitted his scissors into his breast pocket, lowered his spectacles on his nose so he had to tilt his head back to see me, and he erupted into an oration. He spoke disparagingly of small-town yokels who came to college and continued the doldrums of their benighted ways. It was time, he said, for me to become aware, to branch out, to enlarge—to grow up. I was no longer back in the sticks, he said, but had come to the very vortex of culture. No longer would I get my hair cut by the blacksmith, or eat pie with a knife. I should govern myself accordingly. Haircuts, he said, were 35 cents.

So I found Eddie Raymond, who was the other barber and had his shop far down the street in what we would term today the underprivileged part of town. Eddie was born in a back country town far up in Maine called Eagle Lake. The place was first settled by relatives of Evangeline, and fortunately were not known to Longfellow and hence did not get perpetualized in dactyllic hexameter.

Eddie's native tongue, therefore, was an interesting 17th-century French, and at that time he was not much with English. He had come down out of the woods to seek his fortune, having learned to barber in the wilderness, and he made out excellent well on both his fortune and his English, although this is another story. Eddie was still cutting hair for 25 cents and I never paid him more than that all the time he cut mine.

Eddie didn't accompany his work with sophisticated and socially eminent discourse, as did Jud Langen, and it is true that for the extra dime Jud offered a smoother experience. But Eddie could cut hair as well as anybody, even if fastidious customers might have felt his back-country manners uncouth, and his shop sparingly equipped. Eddie would flap the cloth over me, pass clockwise around the chair once, sweep the cloth off, and collect his 25 cents. Besides the dime, this pleased me because I was sooner able to return to my Aeschylus, Plutarch, Dante, Milton, and others of that ilk who were then important. It was fine with Eddie, too, because he could cut about 25 heads an hour and he was making more money than Jud, who because of his higher quality trade had to do some talking.

When Jud finished he would hold up a mirror and the customer would nod, but when Eddie finished he just whisked away the cloth. It was what you were getting, whether you nodded or not. Soon afterwards Eddie saw the feminine trade coming, so he became a *coiffeuse*—although gender is here a small matter to be pondered. He was ahead of everybody, and as a barber for ladies he became well-to-do, went into real estate, and made out fine.

Well, anyway, one time Eddie splashed lather behind my ears to trim my neck, and he had a brush you could use for pasting wallpaper. It felt good, and it was so much larger than the small shaving brush I was using that I inquired about getting one. Eddie said it was a professional model, and the next time the barber supply salesman came in he'd put one down. It cost me $1.35, 1928 values, and it was a real barber's long-spilled Chinese hog bristle shaving brush, six inches of lathering potential. Eddie said he was entitled to a mark-up, but since I was a student he'd let me have it at cost.

Forty years ago, that was. Today a barber is not allowed by Maine law to use a lather brush, and with disruptions in the Orient a Chinese pig is uncooperative. Electric shavers and instant lather are in supply. Unless you own a shaving mug I suppose you'd have trouble finding one. My brush is now about three inches long, but that doesn't mean its time is half done. I don't use it so often, these days. I couldn't get another, so I'm making it last.

1969
Genteel Maneuver

One of the automobile commercials has been using a pleasantly designed young lady in a miniskirt who, to demonstrate the advantages of the new model, has been opening a door and sitting in. The movement is graceful and appealing, and when I guffawed at it my wife asked why. "Because it's some different from getting Aunt Patsy into a buggy," I said.

Aunt Patsy was an ample person whose wildest thoughts never came within a row of apple trees of a miniskirt, and her contour was much like a tarpaulin close-hauled around a load of hay. Getting her in or out of the old one-horse farm buggy was a task, and because I wasn't big enough then to yank or boost I would get the job of holding the horse.

"Turn the wheel and hold the bridle for your Aunt Patsy," they would say, and then everybody would help her in. I know a motion picture of what went on would delight a television audience more than this one of the girl in the miniskirt, but millions of today's viewers would never believe such things happened.

The seat on a farm buggy was just about big enough for two, and if a third person went he would sit on knees. So when Aunt Patsy got in the seat was mainly hers, and whoever drove her around had little room, but the advantage of the high side. Her weight tilted the buggy far to the left, and the driver was about half on the seat and the rest on Aunt Patsy.

If you remember, those buggies had a little step, halfway up from the ground. Ladies gained it at the cost of some modesty, for at least a boot top would be revealed. And just above this little step, and a mite forward, was a roller on the box of the buggy which protected the side against a sharp cut of the front wheel. Which means that by the little step there wasn't much room for getting up and down, and to gain space for larger people there was a trick of geeing the horse. Most farm horses were aware of this, and some would gee by themselves, looking back to see how things went. And for Aunt Patsy we had to gee all we could, and we took no chances.

Mostly, when a gentleman took his lady for a ride, the starting off was a smart and genteel maneuver with a combination of decorum and acrobatics. The gentleman would first get up on the seat, and holding the reins just so would gee the horse. Then he would take the reins in his right hand and holding them thus would place his right hand on the dashboard to steady himself. Next, with his left hand he would reach across and give it to his lady. She, perceiving that all was in readiness, would put her left hand on the dashboard, her left foot on the little step, and she would make a kind of *jeté* which brought her up on the seat gracefully. Then the horse would take off while they were adjusting their laprobe.

But with Aunt Patsy this agile caper became a monumental project. If she ever set her foot on the little step and bore down she would tip the buggy over, so there had to be ballast somewhere. This meant the weight of the driver up on the seat and somebody standing on the opposite step, as well as two husky gentlemen lifting her, one on each arm.

Aunt Patsy had no illusions about her own gorminess, so the deed, although precarious, was done in good humor. She would caution everybody not to hurry the thing, and she would wedge inside the cut-over wheel, hoist one foot to the little step, get everything in readiness, and when she felt the poise and equilibrium were prime she would say, "Now!" Then, up she would go, down would come the left side of the buggy, up would go the driver, and I would let go the bridle and the horse would start.

Mostly, there was no need to hold the bridle, but with Aunt Patsy we always did. Nobody dared surmise what might happen if a chance fly nipped old Fan at the wrong moment, or if in well earned senility old Fan forgot what was going on. So, I always got to hold the bridle for Aunt Patsy, and in those times I was just barely of a size to reach.

She never came except in summer, so I wouldn't have any shoes, and every farm boy knew better than to stand close to a horse when barefoot. From such a posture of safety I, could hardly reach the bridle, and usually I performed with one finger in the bit ring. But this did give me a clear view of the exercises. I was the only one who got to see the show, because everybody else around was pushing, yanking, counter-balancing and fending disaster.

I was the only one who ever saw the pleased look on Aunt Patsy's face as she rode out of the yard, too. The others saw only her back going away, but after I'd dropped the bridle and stood back she would go by me, triumphant. "Thank ye," she would call, and blow me a kiss, and off would go old Fan straining in the tugs. It was a great relief for everybody except old Fan. Why doesn't television have something like that now and then?

1969
Thundershower Picnic

Age cannot wither nor custom stale an only daughter, and the first time Kathy and I went off by ourselves to explore the Maine wilderness was not too different from the hike we had this September—except that I carried her part-way then. I think she was six, but she might have been seven. I know it was before she was eight, because the summer she was eight she undertook to teach a vacationer how to cast a dry fly on the lawn, something she learned with me. "It's all in the w'ist," she kept telling him.

Our special retreat has been Flatiron Pond, high in the hills above Rangeley. It needs an hour's walk to come there, and we set out at daylight. Then we must return to get out of the woods before dark. I carry a packbasket of goodies, and there are always two beefsteaks should the trout be reluctant. Not often have we used the steaks, for Flatiron Pond seldom disappoints.

One year when Kathy was in early high school she attempted a report on our outing for a composition teacher who was not, I fear, worth the liberal emolument promoted by the school committee. Kathy's essay started off, "The place of leaving is the sunrise end of Kennebago Lake, where wispy traces of the night mist still hide the peaks of the West Range. . . ." And so on.

I didn't see it until after the teacher had corrected it, and then I was asked for a fatherly opinion. I found the teacher had changed "place of leaving" to "point of departure," and I looked no farther. I told Kathy our little annual excursion was, after all, something that belonged securely to us, and there would forever be some absurdity in trying to communicate it to *hoi polloi*, including English teachers. Until now I have spared this readership the details on much the same grounds—our point of departure, intermediate stopovers, intervening eventuations, and estimated time of arrival are a timetable of our own, with the special freemasonry of dad and daughter creating all significance.

That first year, when I did no fishing at all but sat with Kathy on my lap so I could guide her little hands and arms as she mastered a nine-foot flyrod, the piscatorial exercises were interrupted each time she succeeded. I daresay, with all the respect to specialists who have other ideas, that the finest eating in the world may be a Flatiron trout slowly and affectionately brought to fruition in deep salt-pork fat over spruce-wood embers on the shore of Flatiron Pond.

So when little Kathy won herself a trout I was obliged to put for shore and cook it. After she had eaten it we would go out and she would win herself another. Before the next year I had inculcated another approach, and since then we have fished all at once, dined all at once and had only one fire.

Another year we had just gained the essential panful when down from Seven Ponds Township came a ripping valley thunderstorm. There is no place I know of where you can get as wet as you can in an open boat in the rain, and we were soaked long before we rowed ashore. "We've lost the tide, so to speak," I said, "and I guess the thing to do is pound the trail for home—dry clothes and a hot oven seem advisable."

"I'm not stepping on that trail until I've had my trout dinner," she said. So we stood there in the rain, lightning and thunder rampant, and we used what weather gear we had to shield our little fire, and when the last trout became a recent memory we walked asquish and adrip back to civilization. People at the point of return told us it was a shame our outing was marred by the storm, but Kathy and I frequently confide to each other that our thundershower picnic was our finest.

This year nothing marred our day. I tied a "grasshopper" on my Thomas rod (I don't let anybody use that except me and Kathy) and handed it to her. She performed the ancient superstitious rite (she spat on the fly) and went to work. Then on an old bungdown bamboo I use only when Kathy has my Thomas, I tied a "professor" and after the same propitiating ceremony I cast away. After I had taken three trouts, and Kathy had none, she suggested that I had unfairly favored myself, and that she perhaps should have a professor, too. To punctuate her sentence there was a choonk, and she had a trout that outweighed my three. After that all merriment was relative.

The sun shone, the hills were serene, the Flatiron trout were amenable. The summercators had gone; even the game warden left us alone. In crepuscular farewell we stood on the trail as the sun moved behind John's Mountain and Flatiron Pond was reddening in a reflection of the sky.

Our little pond was dimpled by rising trouts. We hadn't caught them all; there will be some for next year. Then we returned to the place of leaving and two hours in the truck brought us home to the farm. Here, we found baby Julie had successfully entertained Grandmaw all day without incident, and hadn't missed us. Kathy said to Julie, who isn't old enough yet to lift my Thomas rod, "Some year, you'll go with us."

1970
Just-as-Good-as

So much today is to deplore, but I have just heard about a schoolmarm who teaches just a mite better, and feels she should have praise. She lugs a churn to school once a year and shows her graders how to make butter—something she is able to do because she knows how to, and this may be a criticism of our new-day efforts in general, if one cares to think about it.

Anyway, some years back this teacher realized she was in a communications bind with her little city scholars. She couldn't get across to them because they didn't know what she was talking about.

They were all of the "you can't tell the difference" generation, and in the broad topic of human nutrition and logistics they had no fundamental starting point. The only cow any of them might see would be in a zoo, and even looking at a cow would be hardly instructional to them. Any dairy products they saw or ingested would be machine-tooled and reconstituted until any honest cow, if confronted with her own end result, would blush. The teacher, after thought, decided a churn would be useful.

The one she got is not of the larger kinds once common on the farm, but is a gallon glass jar with eggbeater top, originally meant for the one-cow housewife who wanted merely to crank out butter once a week to keep her menfolks happy. This kind of churn had no commercial intent, and was thus suited for the classroom.

This schoolmarm had made and whacked butter as a girl, but she confirmed her own recollections by asking her mother for a word or two. The mother was once known as the best buttermaker in seven counties, and she not only recited the facts but dug in a kitchen drawer and produced a cream thermometer. The next problem was cream. What do they sell today as cream? Will it churn? How would anybody know? The schoolmarm went to supermarkets until she found a manager who knew what she was talking about, and she bought his cream when he guaranteed it would churn. And as this schoolmarm started to class with her churn, cream, paddle, salt, and buttermold, the mother said, "If it works, bring me the buttermilk."

It worked. Each child watched the warming of the cream, and then took a turn with the crank. Glee attended the "coming," and the bright yellow globules were inspected through the glass. The butter was collected, washed and whacked, and tried both fresh and salted. And afterwards this schoolmarm had her frames of reference.

When you ponder this—the simple churning of a pat of butter—you can only be amazed at the numerous avenues to instruction which it opens. The domestication of animals, agrarian economy, logistics, refrigeration, handling and processing, dictary matters, chemistry and physics, family relations, and the vagaries of technological advancement. Almost the whole human scene may be related, one way or another. I feel this is an unusual schoolmarm.

But we must return now to the mother, who is sitting at home thinking about that buttermilk. It has been long years since she has seen any. Oh, she can reach into any dairy case in any market and bring forth a pasteboard container of "buttermilk." It is cultured, and highly approved on every hand, but in her terms it should be spurned in a society which is otherwise disturbed about truth in advertising, consumer protection, and pollution. It is "just as good as," and thus passes. The mother, of course, knows better, and possibly this explains why this schoolmarm is being cited at this moment.

So after each of the children has had his little lesson about buttermilk, and has had a taste, the schoolmarm carries the churn to her mother, and the mother kicks her heels in the air and shouts hooray, and gets out the big yellow bowl with blue stripes which has slept unused under the shelf since Hector was a pup. She splashes flour around, and she makes a big pan of buttermilk biscuits. These would melt in your mouth, and they were so light and feathery they had to lay a plate on them so they wouldn't fly away. Numerous remarks and comments followed, only one of which I shall report: the schoolmarm said, "A good teacher always gets so much more than she gives."

The greatest lesson for us, from all this, is that true buttermilk, as distinguished from the kind made on a turret-lathe, has chemical properties which, in the heat of the oven, act upon the baking soda in a correct and inspired manner. Cultured buttermilk, while just-as-good-as, always leaves a sody taste in buttermilk biscuits. It is even so, but I doubt if any teachers' college has a churn in the techniques lab. As Marcus Aurelius said, "Cultured buttermilk ain't worth a hoot in a biscuit." The translation is my own.

1971
Sycophant of Sedentary Comfort

Researchers at Kiel University, after long and expensive experiment, have devised a new kind of electric chair. This one is not for executions. It has an even 60 buttons, each about three inches in diameter and looking like a toadstool, on which the customer will adjust his anatomy. Pressure on each button, three-inch portion by three-inch portion, communicates by electronic impulse to create a picture on a television screen. The news release explains that by watching this picture, and seeing just how a posterior is disposed, a manufacturer of furniture can design something better than we now sit on. What interests me, mostly, is that the framework on which the Kiel researchers have mounted their buttons looks very much like my old Morris chair.

I surmise that some people, including the Kiel professors, may not know, today, what a Morris chair is, or was, and that as a sycophant of sedentary comfort I should make harangue. Else, of course, these mad Germans will perfect some monstrosity which, regardless of its fit, computes into perfect pleasure.

Nobody, I believe, can improve on a Morris chair, and its lamented disappearance from the furniture stores not only impugns the intelligence of buyers and sellers, but explains why these Kielers are groping for the beautiful dream—if they knew about Morris chairs, or could buy one, they wouldn't be trying to make one.

William Morris, 1834 to 1896, had a versatile talent. Having translated Homer and Vergil into English verse, he took up Icelandic sagas, meantime running a printing plant, doing paper hanging and decorating, and running a furniture factory. He is credited with changing the home furnishing taste of the British people, and thinking the English had been settled in an uncomfortable posture quite long enough, he offered his Morris chair—a simple enough affair with an adjustable back and large cushions which, somehow, he was able to devise without the aid of electronic foofaraw.

The Morris chair was a fast seller. Up until about World War I every home of sensitivity had one, or more. They were the favorites of the older folks (senior citizens) until one would become established as Uncle's Chair, or Grampie's Chair, and whoever was poaching was expected to rise and vacate if the owner arrived. When a rightful owner was duly installed, a joy of childhood was to climb on his lap and cuddle for a story. Too much sentiment has been wasted on the rocking chair—it was the Morris chair that invited repose and coddled the anatomy.

The bug in the Morris chair was the weft of burlap straps under the seat cushion, and this small fault probably sent the invention into desuetude. These straps, supporting the cushion, were tacked to the frame, and the tacks were never substantial enough to endure. One day, sooner or later, the housekeeper would sweep up a tack, and it was time to make repairs or fall through.

We have two. One is a plain, inexpensive model made of birch. The other is heavy mission oak, scrolled, and thrusting out front legs carved into lion's paws, like an ancient cast-iron bathtub. I find both equally comfortable, but tend to motion visitors into the ornate one, noblesse oblige. I have had people come to talk, and seen them doze before the argument got hot.

In time, that part of the frame of every Morris chair was tacked and retacked to shreds, until there was no more strength in the wood to hold more tacks. Plastic Wood came too late to serve and save the Morris chair.

Both these chairs had been relegated to the attic, their tack bars riddled, their burlap hanging, and their backs tipped down so both cushions could be set on top. One had lost its metal rod for adjusting, and the grooves for the rod were broken away. My grandmother, my mother, my wife, and my daughter had all said, one time or another, "We ought to get those chairs fixed."

Not knowing that such endeavor, at Kiel University, is under research, I lugged them down and fixed them. I didn't use Plastic Wood, but rebuilt the frames to start fresh with sound places to tack. It was eight years, as I figure, before the Morris bug appeared, and a loose tack was swept from under. I have repaired and renewed faithfully, and both Morris chairs are in good shape right now and do not want for patronage. "Oh, what an interesting old chair!" say some, and others say, "Wherever did you find a Morris chair?" The cat, you may like to know, prefers the simple one, and when I roust him down so I may privilege myself he gives me a dirty look.

I have a comfortable feeling, roughly from the back of my knees to the hinder part of my neck, that the professors of Kiel and all their research will do nothing better than William Morris did. Unless they can figure out something to do about those tacks.

1972
"Going to Haul"

For going-on a week, I've been waking promptly at 2:45 a.m. I don't get up, but I look at the luminous dial, say, "Good luck, Harold!" and go back to sleep. One swallow doesn't make a summer, but one trip to haul seems to make that much of a lobsterman out of a highlander.

Harold Jameson is a lobsterman, and for some time he had been saying, "You ought to get up some morning and go haul with me!" So long as it was "some morning" I was agreeable, but now Harold said, "I'll pick you up tomorrow." I set my alarm at 2:45, Harold tooted his pick-up at 3:00, and we were off down Muscongus Bay to attend 65 traps in the vicinity of Mosquito Rock. I will be glad when I get this 2:45 stuff out of my system.

Maine lobstermen are not the heave-ho and breaking-wave kind of mariner. They respect their ocean to the point of timidity. It has been said the men who never fear the sea are its victims; the cautious and prudent give it never a chance. The reason for pre-dawn hauling of lobster pots is in tune with this—on the long average the Maine ocean is calmest on the tail of night and before the morning breezes up. Each day's decision about "going to haul" is made in the darkness on the wharf, so after sniffing and with many a "waal, I dunno," Harold decided "mebbe" it would hold calm long enough to get his 65 traps by Mosquito Rock.

Mosquito Rock is some seven miles "outside." This was the morning of May 29, so the full moon was a day old, and it didn't hurt the scenery a mite. Harold had his running lights on, and had tuned in the fishermen's band on his two-way radio. We were not alone on the ocean, and it was fun to listen to the chit-chat of lobstermen like us, on their way out. We rounded a can at the harbor mouth, came through a channel between islands, and picked up the lights of Port Clyde on our left, the lights of Pemaquid on our right, and 15 miles straight ahead the Monhegan Island lighthouse. Revolving at 30-second intervals, it became Harold's course, and his engine thrummed musically. He figured an hour and a half to sunrise. Not quite that to Mosquito Rock.

Harold is what we Mainers call an "old woman." This has nothing to do with sex, but means a devotion to detail. A place for everything and everything in its place. Other fishermen will tell you he isn't a "fahst" hauler, but will admit his methodical routine saves him time and effort. As we approached Mosquito Rock he began getting ready. A tub of alewives was disposed by his left foot, and he threaded three on his bait iron—a long steel needle. He laid his spectacles on a shelf—hauling would spray them opaque instantly. He set out his box of wooden pegs, which render lobster claws clampless, and tossed in his gauge— Maine lobsters must all be legal lengths. Then he hauled on his neoprene fisherman's pants—an exhibition of agility in a rolling boat considering that he was already wearing his hip rubber boots. "There," he said, and we began looking for his first pink- and-green pot buoy.

A Maine lobster trap is a slatted crate that lies on the ocean floor. The line to it is called a pot-warp, and at Mosquito Rock Harold fishes in 30 fathoms of water. A few feet above the trap is a plastic float that keeps the line from snarling about the trap. A second float is called the toggle, and its purpose is to take up slack when the tide ebbs. The third float, on the end of the warp, is the pot-buoy, and this is painted in bright colors in each fisherman's distinctive marking. The toggle may or may not be under water, but as we were on a slack tide it was now floating, and Harold gaffed his lines by the toggle. Out of 65, he missed once, and he turned to see if I noticed his clumsiness. It was the look Esposito had that night he muffed the easy one.

Maneuvering the boat to come alongside each toggle was, of course, routine with Harold, but the skill and beauty of it was exciting. Having no precious lobster license, I couldn't help him, so I watched him do his work according to his usual lone- someness. They tell me Harold doesn't ask "just anybody" to go hauling with him. With his bait iron threaded, he was ready for number one. Up came the toggle, he made a turn on his winch, he adjusted his motor controls, threw the knob on his winch, and the warp tightened. When the pot "breeched," he grabbed it, pulled it into position, adjusted his controls again, and in seconds he had taken out his lobsters, cleaned away the crabs, winkles, old bait, and had transferred the new alewives to the bait string in the trap. Watching his depth finder, he swung about to put the trap back in the ocean just where he wanted it. Then, approaching his next trap, he rethreaded his bait iron, measured his catch, and hove back all but the "keepers." He caught hundreds of lobsters, but only 44 from the 65 traps were legal to bring ashore. At $1.40 a pound, he paid for his bait, his fuel, and pocketed some $60, much of which would go to amortizing his boat and gear.

It was noon when we came to the wharf, and 1:00 p.m. when I had breakfast. Harold does this every day, but it threw my highlander schedules askew. Now, every morning when I awake at 2:45 a.m., and before I turn over, I meditate briefly on what a good time I had with him, and console myself that a farmer's life isn't so bad in some ways.

1973
Distance Diminishes
Delecstasy

Our Food Page said, "The challenge of cooking fresh-caught fish scares off many an inexperienced chef." The article then gives recipes for delectable sauces for fresh-caught fish, made with olives, avocado, and yogurt, whatever that is. "Olives, yogurt, and avocado mix into savory condiments," it said.

This is undoubtedly a good thing to know, but I do not plan to burden my packbasket with such delights on any trout expedition in the near future, particularly since there are few wilderness facilities to accommodate the instructions, "Cover and chill one or more hours." Fresh-caught fish, to me, means one chap making a fire so it will be ready when the other chaps come ashore with the catch. This treatise on fresh fish made me think of the time Buddie Russell won his title of World's Champion Outdoor Cook at the big celebration when Bangor was recalling her glorious past.

Bangor was the boom town of the lumbering days, and a wilderness theme prevailed. The committee related the new interest in patio and picnic cooking to the early woods cooking of camp and drive, and offered good prizes as well as the title. It really was an international competition, as somebody came down from Canada and another man had his hibachi and an Oriental menu. But it was evident early that the real contest was among three Maine guides, one of them Buddie, who represented the Rangeley Lakes Region.

Buddie deployed his wangan early in the forenoon, as did the other contestants, each in his own roped-off area on the fair grounds. He kindled his little fire. I forget what-all he prepared, but somewhere in the beginning he had a lobster bisque. His fish course was matched Flatiron Pond trouts, each exactly 14 inches long, and all taken on a barbless Kennebago Wulff with a two-ounce rod. His main dish was a seven-rib roast of beef. Then he baked biscuits, turned out a loaf of warm bread, nurtured his vegetables, and I remember he made wild-blueberry pancakes which served both as appetizer and dessert. It was his trout course which prompts this flash-back.

The judges for this world-shaking competition, five in number, had been carefully selected. One was a charming lady from France who was gourmet culinary editor of some gastronomical publication of high repute in that nation of high cuisine. This was her first visit to Maine, and she had never seen our *Salvelinus f. fontinalis*, or brook trout. In Flatiron Pond (elevation 1975 ft., area 0.04 sq. mis.) these beasties attain peculiar beauty because of the cold water, and their flesh has its own tint so that anybody who knows can tell a Flatiron fish from the same variety taken elsewhere. This lady from France, judge's clipboard in hand, looked over the rope and watched Buddie panfrying his beauties.

"But," she said, "You are making a *souse*, n'est-ce pas?"

"A what?" says Buddie.

"A sauce, for ze feesh."

"Not for these fish, I ain't," and the "ain't" indicated Buddie was playing things to the hilt, because he doesn't talk that way otherwise.

Epicures well know that any fish available in France requires some kind of Cordon Bleu garnish to make it palatable, and that for the most part when French fish is pronounced delicious it is always the sauce, and not the flesh, that merits the praise. This lady had never taken a fish that wasn't lubricated with something in the olive-yogurt-avocado genre, and Buddie's trout looked naked as they approached their supreme moment.

Recipe: Dice a sufficient quantity of salt pork and render it over a slow fire. There should be maybe a half inch of fat in the frypan. The crisp nuggets of salt pork may be retrieved about the time the fresh fish come ashore, as they have other uses, but some leave them. Dress the trouts at water's edge and lave them in the pond water. Roll them lightly in cornmeal. Insert them gently in the pork fat, and do not have the fat too hot as they will curl. If they commence to curl, turn them at once. Cook slowly, and baste carefully. As they approach doneness, the cook will need a club to hold off his companions. Sans sauce, such trouts are eaten close to the fire, and the fire is close to the shore, as distance diminishes delecstasy. The lady judge had two of Buddie's trouts, expressed gustatory delight, made notes on her clipboard, but kept saying, "Pas de sauce, tch, tch!"

She gave Buddie points on his fish course, but awarded top score to a guide from Jo-Mary Lake who had split an eight-pound Moosehead landlock salmon and had broiled it before, not over, a cedar fire. He didn't make a sauce either. He'd tell you, as I do, that here in Maine the word "sauce" means applesauce, or preserved fruits served in a sauce dish for dessert. Our

trout and salmon need no olives, yogurt, and avocado, whatever that is.

1974
Popcorn without Butter

Young William and his Gramp went on a picnic Friday, and
we closed the generation gap so you can't even see the
crack—but we had the terrible disappointment of no butter. William is now four and fiving fast, so he no longer clouds up and
storms if he falls down, and taking him to the woods has no
babysitting problems for Gramp. We made out like two old cro-
nies off on a time, and except for the lack of butter everything
was a hundred percent. It was a major oversight, and we
decided to give "Gam" what-for the moment we got home. She
packed the wangan.

The timber operation in our woods was now well under way,
so I had sent word that if William might be spared I would con-
duct him through the cutting. He had come with new boots and
a new skidoo suit, and bowed down by admonitions to be a
good boy, mind Gramp, and not whimper if occasion arose. The
wangan was packed in the Kennebecker, and the Kennebecker
in the box on the moosesled along with William, and with many
a gay giddyap I hauled the load through the fields, over the
knoll, and into the woods. The choppers were already at work,
and we could hear the saws and the skidder. We even heard a
tree come down as we approached Camp Willy—which is our
snug little cabin by the sugarhouse. Then we started a fire in the
stove, arranged our wangan on the table, filled the kettle at the
spring, and walked over to the cutting.

I was about William's age when my grandfather took me on the same trip. I saw them working the crosscut saws and watched the trees come down. I saw them yank out the logs with oxen, and roll them from the brow onto sleds to go to the mill. At noontime we hunkered by an open fire against a boulder and ate a stew that Gramp had made in a pail, and some hot biscuits he had baked in another. But everything has changed. The crosscut is gone until many of today's choppers have never seen one, and the chainsaw howls in its place. Cleat-tractors skid tree-length logs from the woods, and nobody rolls, or cants, logs today. A derricklike loader piles them on trucks, and ten yokes of oldtime oxen couldn't start one of the loads. And now we have a tight camp for noontime, with a stove that has an oven. So we spent the forenoon at forestry, and came to the camp to find it warm with the kettle steaming—our intention to encourage nourishment and demolish the wangan. This is when we discovered the lack of butter.

It was easy to see how Gam had failed us. She had tucked in a big jar of peanut butter, and William and I are not averse to this as a substitute up to a point—that point being popcorn. All morning I had been promising William a blast of popcorn, and as we stood and looked at the peanut butter we could see that Gam had failed us. We had agreed that we would have all the popcorn to eat that we wanted, and then we would put what was left by the spring for the chickadiddles and the adjidaumos. William and I suspected that the chickadiddles and adjidaumos might just as lief have peanut butter, but that we wouldn't. We'd liefer have butter.

The popcorn, of course, was ceremonial. We needed it about the way we needed ballet slippers. The wangan was supreme, and we even had a cup of hot soup for a starter. But we weren't working up to the intended climax. The kettle singing on the stove proved that we could pop corn just fine, but what was the sense?

William gave the matter good thought, and came up with a solution. He said, "We'll just eat it without butter!" So after we ate the pie, and finished up all the milk, we got the sheet-iron popcorn popper off its nail, and we tossed in a handful—my handful, because my hand is bigger'n William's. Agitation being applied, we soon had the finest popper of corn you ever saw or smelled. And using no lubrication, we just sifted on the salt and took our chances. It wasn't bad, but we favor butter. There wasn't much left for the chickadiddles and the adjidaumos, but we made the gesture.

Then we washed up the dishes so they'd be clean when we came again, dumped out the kettle so it wouldn't freeze and burst, swept the floor, filled the woodbox, and brought the moosesled home—William again in command of the fleet team. The sled tipped over only once, which is pretty good logging, but at another place William decided to get off and walk a ways just in case. When we got home he really gave Gam what-for. "You," he said, "did a terrible thing to us men! You forgot butter in the wangan!"

"But I put in peanut butter instead," she said.

William said, "For popcorn?"

So Gam was sorry and promised it would never happen again.

Glossary:

Wangan—the picnic; groceries and supplies.

Kennebecker—a knapsack; in this instance a pack basket.

Moosesled—a wide, good-sized handsled for toting in the woods. Sometimes called a handshark.

Chopper—anybody who cuts a tree, even though he uses a saw.

Brow—a loading ramp of logs from which logs are moved onto the vehicle.

1975
The Greatest Thing since Sliced Bread

The subject being table manners, Fritz Hartman writes from California to recall how to get a slice of bread when the bread plate is at the other end of the table. He says, "You didn't ask to have the plate passed to you. Instead, you passed your fork and asked someone to stab you a slice." In amplification of that, it *was* genteel to take bread with a fork, because I've seen it done. I've seen other things done with bread, too, and pea soup, baked beans, and molasses come to mind.

The kind of bread in context was called "casting bread" for a reason now mostly lost. Bread was baked daily in the Maine lumber camps. Cookee mixed his wet ingredients in a bowl, and then dumped them into his barrel of flour. The moisture would take up the proper quantity of flour and then Cookee would "cast" his dough onto the kneading board. Lumber-camp bread was mostly a salt rising kind, and it was delicious the day it was baked. Overnight, though, it would set up like cement. The loaves were huge, so a slice of bread might be a foot across. Cookee sliced the loaves and had platters of slices along the tables.

Lacking refrigeration and regular supply, a cook of the old breed depended on foods that wouldn't spoil, and split peas and baking beans were reliables. Every meal began with a dollop of pea soup, which a man could refuse if he wished none. Cookee passed along the tables with a pot and a ladle, and the soup was put on the flat dinner plate. Soup flexible enough to run far was not admired. The soup was sopped with a slice of bread and thus eaten out of hand.

Baked beans are still called "logging berries" in the Maine woods. They were baked in a big iron pot in a beanhole. Since the covering could not be disturbed until the cooking was done, the pot had to have enough water to last all the way, and bean-hole beans were always juicy. When a chopper had forked his helping of beans, he would reach for another slice of bread and swab his plate.

It was not lumber-camp custom to pass a fork for bread. Wanting some, a chopper merely said, "Bread." It was passed to him, or Cookee brought it. But while a man could ask for something, he could not discuss it. Conversation was forbidden. This was to speed the meal, and it avoided arguments that might arise over differences of opinions—arguments often leading to worse. The ban also spared Cookee any comments about his food.

Molasses, in those days, was much used for all sweetening. Maine's seafaring experiences had made the state partial to West Indies products, and Barbados molasses was favored. This heavy, dark treacle came in hogsheads, and a lumber-camp dingle would have several horsed up to last the winter. Cookee used it to sweeten the baked beans, and in all his pies, cakes, cookies, and puddings. In addition, jugs were kept on the tables, and after a man had had his fill of desserts, he would pour molasses on his plate and dip a slice of bread in it. Molasses was believed to be quick energy for strong men doing heavy work in below-zero weather.

There is a story about the time "King" Lacroix went to Philadelphia. This storied Canadian was a sort of Paul Bunyan in the Eagle Lake region of Maine. He put up at the finest hotel in the city, and went into the dining room for supper. After he finished eating, he picked up his dishes after the lumber-camp custom and carried them "to the sink." Every chopper takes his dishes to the sink. Accordingly Lacroix arrived in the hotel kitchen, where he complained to a flabbergasted chef that there had been no molasses on his table.

Thank you, Fritz.

1976
What Ever Happened to Marbles?

"What ever happened to my marble bag?" I asked, and my wife said, "Didn't you give it to Bill?" Maybe I did, and I hope he doesn't play for keeps until he has mastered a few maneuvers essential to marble prosperity. There were some peewees left in the bag, and I notice the stores don't offer them now. The only marbles I've seen for sale for years have been glass ones, and probably the real clay marbles of time-that-was belong only to keepsaking grandpaws and grand-sons thereof.

There would be a boy now and then whose momma had for-bidden him to play for keeps, but I think this approach to open gambling had less to do with the matter than pure penny-pinch-ing. She was probably a mother who didn't see marbles in their true light, and thought losing one was squandering. The things cost ten for a cent, so the hazard wasn't huge, and a boy with reasonably nimble fingers could do a lot of marbling without going-home-a-crying. I made out best with my own invention—a pasteboard shoe box with holes in it. If the hole had a "5" beside it, I paid five marbles to any boy who rolled a marble through that hole, keeping all that missed for myself. The holes were different sizes and the biggest pay-off was ten—but that hole was calibrated so you wouldn't believe it. After a half dozen boys had rolled fifty marbles apiece at my box, I would pay off fifteen or twenty marbles without a squawk.

Marbles came out as soon as the frost was gone on the south side of the schoolhouse, and we could twist our heels in the ground to make a bunny hole. I never cared much for bunny-in-the-hole, because it ran to a good handful of marbles on one pitch. Everybody up, and the boy who tossed the most marbles into the bunny hole took all. So fortunes were won and lost each recess, and bunny-in-the-hole seemed to me a lot like shooting off a five dollar skyrocket. That's the fastest way to spend money that I know of.

The peewee was a shooter, and in those days a glass marble was called an "aggie" and was used only for a target. When a boy got low on peewees, he could "set up" an aggie and other boys pitched at it until it got hit. The successful boy now owned the aggie, but the original owner had all the peewees that missed. Aggies cost real money. Sometimes a boy would shoot and shoot, hoping to win an aggie, until his peewees dropped close to bankruptcy, and then with a stroke of skill he would connect. Now he could set up his aggie and hope to recoup. He would be sad if some low character popped on the button the first shot. Hearts are broken in many ways.

The peewee was merely a clay pellet fired in a kiln, and peewees came in assorted colors. If a warm spring day brought showers and a boy got soaked to the skin, he would sit in school and a streak of composite dye would ooze down from his marble pocket. After that, all his marbles were the same color.

I'm sure marbles are played today, else the stores wouldn't have the glass ones. But I'm sure, too, that like much else, things aren't the same. That ten-for-a-cent marbles were fairly easy to come by, either by purchase or by skill, made it possible for a boy to accumulate quite a pocketful, so that cheapness had a value. Such wealth made quite a stir when it rolled out of a pocket during joggerfy class. This happened often enough, and teachers were graded, term to term, by the way they reacted to this. We loved those who understood, and said, "Now, Willis, pick them up and don't let that happen again." But those who confiscated the marbles and kept them in a desk drawer until school closed in June were no ornament to education, and a boy with his marbles in teacher's desk was bereft. I hear people say, "He's lost his marbles," and it means something else now. It was far sadder back when it meant marbles. When I lost my marbles, in joggerfy class, I asked Mother to sew me up a bag, so I never had that problem again. That's the bag Grandson Bill may or may not have. With a few peewees.

1977
What's in a Name, Anyway?

Whent we had our foliage vacation we underwrote a motel at Dumfries, New Brunswick, and the young woman who discounted our money looked up from our registration card and said, "Friendship—what a good name for a town!" It is, but I explained that Maine has had a thing about abstractions, and we also have a Liberty, a Union, a Hope, a Freedom, a Harmony, a Strong, and a Unity where two brothers are said to dwell together, Bill and Roscoe. But behold—we also have a Misery Gore.

A gore is an irregular section of land left over after surveying, sometimes being a mistake, and is one of many words used in Maine for a place, others being town, addition, corner, grant, landing, purchase, surplus, location, and even survey. Misery Gore is a wild land township in Somerset County, adjacent to Jackman.

As we rode along after that I began reviewing Maine place

names, and since coming home I have checked the several authorities, and the subject is mildly fascinating. I'd rather go on a picnic, but lacking other diversion:

Maine has places named Washington, Adams, Jefferson, Madison, Monroe, Jackson, Van Buren, Harrison, Tyler, Taylor, Pierce, Lincoln, Johnson, Grant and Grant's (Simpson Academy Grant and Grant's at Kennebago), Hayes, Garfield, Cleveland, McKinley, Taft, Wilson, Harding's, Kennedy, Nixon, and Ford. We lack Polk, Fillmore, Buchanan, Arthur, Roosevelt, Coolidge, Hoover, Truman, and Eisenhower.

We have Springvale, Summerset, Island Falls, and Winterport. We have two Saturday Ponds and one Sunday River, but are otherwise weak in that category. We have a couple of Mile Brooks, but one is a mile and a quarter long and the other over three miles. One Mile Brook is three miles long, and Two Mile Brook is twelve and a half. But things even out when Nine Mile Brook is only four miles, and Twentyfivemile Brook is only eleven.

There was a custom of naming townships for foreign and Biblical places, and we have a lot of those without any particular reference to the originals. Norway was not settled by Norwegians. In fact, Vienna isn't even Vienna—the Maine pronunciation is vighenny. Athens, Belfast, Bremen (say breem'n), Brunswick, Calais (say cal-l's), Canton, Carmel, Carthage, China, Denmark, Frankfort, Levant, Lisbon, Madrid, Mexico, Moscow, Naples, Paris, Peru, Poland, Rome, Smyrna, Troy, Verona, and Wales.

We have a Sunset, a Sunrise, and an Aurora. Biblical names include Bethel, Canaan, Corinth, Gilead, Hebron, Hiram, Jerusalem, Lebanon, and the religious colony of Frank Sandford that fell into disrepute earlier in the century was called Shiloh and it stood on Beulah Hill.

In a state that freely uses ancient Indian names, two words sometimes beguile—Piscataquis and Piscataqua. Well, after Kennebago, Cupsuptic, Mattawamkeag, Passadumkeag, Macwahoc, Mooselookmeguntic, and Umbagog, one may be pardoned if he assumes Piscataquis and Piscataqua are Indian. The Latin dictionary explains under *piscatus* and *aqua*.

We have some 35 Beaver Ponds (plus, of course, unnumbered beaver ponds), about as many Long Ponds and Long Coves and Long Islands, and a slew of Pleasant Brooks, Coves, Islands, Lakes, Mountains, Ponds, and Points. We have 65 Mud Ponds and 14 Mud Lakes. Many of these are clear, sparkling water, and the best way to explain this nomenclature is to consider Maine whimsy and the fact that a beautiful body of water has been called Dry Pond—we have three Dry Ponds in Maine.

As for Friendship, some say it was named after the friendliness of the people. Perhaps, but another story is that early inhabitants were badly used by the Indians, and disliked perpetuating the Indian name of Medumcook. One day a coastal sloop visited Medumcook Harbor, and on her transom she bore: FRIENDSHIP. "That'd be a good name for our town," said somebody, and he proved to be accurate.

1978
Singing Along . . .

M usic hath charms, and some friends who lately made the Allagash canoe trip came home singing an improbable song. "Everybody sings that!" they explained, and the tune ran in their heads for a week or more, causing them to burst forth anon. If I recall rightly, it was in 1960 that this melodic custom began, and we have reason to know. We were three couples, three canoes, and we wanted a last happy vacation on the lovely waterway before the preservationists took it over to spoil the fun. That's right; none of us has been there since.

We "put in" at Telos Lake, and had twenty-two miles of paddling before our first camp at Lock Dam. We let Flats Jackson
take the lead, as he is an ancient riverman and could teach us
by example. The day was perfectly calm, a breeder that proved
itself with a torrential easterly the next day. A little behind Flats
and inshore was our second canoe, and I was the same distance
behind but farther out in the lake. We hadn't much more than
got under way, taking the positions we would hold all day,
when ol' Flats burst into song.

Flats has a beautiful tenor voice. Many's the time we've joined
him around camp fires. Now, he let go in the magnificent morning with, "You had a dream dear . . ."

> He kept right on: "I had one too . . .
> "Mine was the best dream, because
>> it
>>> was
>>> of
>> you . . "

We didn't join him in this rendition. It would have spoiled
things. Behind us Mount Katahdin was prominent, ahead of us
lay unruffled Chamberlain Lake. Sky and water were so very
blue. No sound in the wilderness save Flats's good tenor, and
we listened. "Come, Sweetheart, tell me—now is the tim-m-m-
e . . ." Flats finished the song.

We laid our paddles across the gunwhales and clapped
hands. Beautiful! But Flats paid no attention to this appreciation;
he kept his ol' guide's stroke and began the song again; "I had
a dream dear, you had one too. . . ."

Well, you see, Flats was using the ballad like the Song of the
Volga Boatmen, or any sea chantey, and he was stroking his
paddle to the tune. All day long, with just a pause for lunch
ashore, he kept singing—over and over, and we quickly realized
that this was the finest song to paddle by. Bow and stern, the
rhythm suited, and along we went—because in short order we
were singing with Flats—and we chopped off the long miles of

Chamberlain Lake as neatly as anybody has ever.

We saw nobody else until we got to Lock Dam, and here was a trim scoutmaster with a supervised group, and they stood at attention along the sand as we nosed in. "Quite a chorale you have there!" he called pleasantly. "We've been listening ever since you rounded Nugent's point."

That next day it stormed. Nobody moved on the river and lakes, and it wasn't too much fun to stand around biding under a wet spruce tree. But the wind eased off at dusk, the rain stopped, and in a bright sunrise we carried over to Eagle Lake to resume our trip and the singing of Flats. We went to The Tramway, and then to Ziggler's Campground ("Mine was the best dream because it was of you, Come, Sweetheart tell me . . .") and after we had set up camp for that night we heard the bunch of Boy Scouts arriving from Lock Dam.

In perfect tempo, every paddle rising and falling together, they came into earshot:

> "You tell me your dream . .
> I'll tell you mine. . . ."

The Boy Scouts went down the river before we did, so the establishment of a traditional Allagash River Canoe Song can be blamed on them. As we followed, a day or so behind, everybody we met was singing "I had a dream dear, you had one too. . . ."

And now our friends, who say the restrictions and regulations imposed by the authorities who now control the waterway in the public interest are somewhat unamusing, are back and they are singing our song. The Allagash Song. They say only what Flats Jackson knew all the time—it's the best paddling tune there is.

1979
Who Remembers the Lard Pail?

C ook said if I'd fetch her some lard, she'd make me a blueberry pie. In mid-winter I'd rather have that than a
license to steal, so I brought a bag of blueberries from the freezer
and went to Fales Mkt. for some lard. "No got," said the buy,
who is given to picking up oddities from the summer people.

"No lard?"

"Nope."

"Is there some reason for this deplorable destitution in a land
otherwise flowing with milk and honey?" It takes a certain
amount of effort to counteract the seasonal sloppiness, and
when it comes to language I can hold up my end.

"I dunno," he said. "We order it all the time, but none
comes."

"So how is my wife going to make me a blueberry pie?"

He pointed at several just-as-goods on the shelf, things I had
seen well recommended on the TV, all of them non-this and
non-that and made from wonderful things that are good for me.
I said, "My wife still makes her pie crust from lard, and I have
every intention of protecting her in this abysmal ignorance."

So I went to some other places, and in the third one I found
lard. She performed as agreed, and that blueberry pie was some
old good.

Evidently lard is not supplied indifferently, as the demand
has waned. There is no substitute in pie crust for pure, old-time

leaf lard, and this should be embroidered in letters of gold and hung on the august walls of the Smithsonian Institution.

Who remembers the lard pail?

Lard could be had "loose"; it came in a tub and the grocer dipped it by the pound. Or it could be had in a pail—two-pound, three-pound, and five-pound. These were substantial tin pails with tight covers and sturdy bails, and after the lard had been worked into the family program they had a thousand uses until they wore out. The lard pail disappeared from the domestic grocery long since, but for some time afterwards it persisted up in Canada. The Canadian pail had a bright red maple leaf as a trade mark, and before busing you could look a mile ahead up the roads and see scholars with their maple-leaf pails carrying their lunches to school. That was before hot lunches, too. It was grand to visit Canada and see all the lucky people who still had lard pails.

I had a two-pound pail for my school lunch, but I was a light eater. Two-three sandwiches, a cold chicken leg, pickles, cupcakes, pie, cookies, and an apple, and I was ready to run outside and play. I remembered the Willard twins had a ten-pound pail—the hotel model—but they usually had a sandwich or two for recess instead of waiting for noonin'.

The lard pail was great for berrying. Loop your belt through the handle, and both hands were free to pick.

It was just right for picking up the hens' eggs.

We had one for well water. The deep well in the field had the best water in town, so we always lowered a lard pail just before each meal and had the freshest water. Sometimes gentility tipped the pail into a pitcher, but there was nothing gauche about setting the lard pail on the table.

Now and then Mother would send us with a small gift of cookies to a shut-in or some older neighbor having a birthday. She'd hand us the lard pail with the goodies, and we'd set out in the pleasant spirit of a good deed. We might go in if we were asked in, she would say, but behave yourselves and mind your manners, and don't wear out your welcome. We might never have mastered the amenities if it weren't for the lard pail! Then she would call after us, "And don't forget to bring home that lard pail! I couldn't keep house without it!"

People seem to be able to today, and can even do it without lard.

Too bad.

1980
Whistling Memories

E ddie Skillin and I were of an age, and shared many happy boyhood adventures. We had our own whistle. We thought we were using the lovely song of the wood thrush, but years afterward we learned that we had appropriated the first four notes of "*O Canada.*" When we were boys the Canadian anthem was "*The Maple Leaf Forever*" and we didn't know anything about "*O Canada*"—no more did the wood thrush. When Eddie whistled under my window I'd hurry out to find what he had in mind, and he'd do the same for me. I suppose we presumed everybody else would think a wood thrush was about.

One of the best things Eddie and I did was to hike off the last week or so of summer vacation and tent out. We'd plan to be home just in time to shine up and report. Hitchhiking was yet to be invented, so we walked out and we walked back. We had a World War pup tent, made of two pieces that buttoned at the ridge, and Eddie had one piece and I had the other. Come late afternoon we'd button our tent, hang it on a piece of potwarp between two trees, and make a fir or hemlock mattress. Our late summer excursions came after the black fly plague had subsided, but we did fight a lot of mosquitoes. Between our two packsacks we had everything we needed.

One year we were walking up the Sebasticook River and made camp at an ideal spot. In the morning, as we made our breakfast over our little fire, Eddie poked in the sand and picked up an arrow point. We became archaeologists on the spot, and that forenoon gathered eight pounds of flint relics from the Stone Age. The weight was established by the postmaster at Harmony, because we mailed the artifacts home in a box. We were rather pleased with ourselves for choosing that campsite— a spot that had been used thousands of years before us for the same reason we use it: it was the right place if you came along. Prehistoric people had paused there, as we had, and probably a worker in flint did business with them. Not all the points we found were good ones, but some were, and two-three of them are in museums. Eddie's father, something of a gem buff, made a few of them into pendants on golden chains, and I think my sister still has one.

There was a crisp winter night, another time, when Eddie ripped off our whistle under my window, and I stuck my head up from under my pile of blankets to wonder what would bring him out in the chill. It took me a time to get into my high-cuts and my winter hefties, and I came out our back door to find Eddie on the steps. "Northern lights!" he said, and I looked up to see the firmament afire. We trudged in the hip-deep snow out behind our buildings, to blank out a streetlamp down the way, and for the next hour or so saw one of the finest displays of its kind in my time. We stood a short ladder against the hen-house and went up on the roof. There wasn't much pitch to one side, so we lay back in the snow and had a perfect view. There was the green glow in the north, with the waving streamers of various colors passing up and over. The waves did pass over, and lighted the sky to the south of us, which we had never seen before. The 45th parallel north latitude runs across Maine, so that meant our spectacle was reaching halfway to the equator. Quite a show.

We stayed backs down in the snow for some time after the show was over. As the lights simmered down, the sky became dark again, and the stars grew brighter. But the show finally ended, and we came down the ladder. Eddie went home and I went up to my room to find my snug blankets had cooled off while I was away and I had the job of warming them again. That took a little while, and before my teeth stopped chattering I had rerun the northern lights many times. Why do you suppose it is that whenever I hear somebody sing "*O Canada*" before an ice hockey game I think of the northern lights?

When I came home from school the next day, my father said, "I give up—maybe you can solve the big mystery."

"What do you know about some jokers who climbed onto my henhouse and bedded down in the snow?"

The evidence of our supine observations did seem hard to believe in the daylight. My father was greatly relieved at my simple explanation.

1981
Harold's Duck Takes a Bow

I guess I'll tell about Harold's duck. Just a year ago I sang, told, and related how a mallard hen came off the wild Atlantic flyway to nest in the forward house of Harold's lobster boat, *Blossom*. At that time, *Blossom* was moored in Friendship harbor, as Harold hadn't set any traps to begin his summer's fishing. But he was getting ready, checking his gear, and as he half stood up toward the bow he looked eyeball to eyeball with this lady and he was much astonished. Nobody ever heard of a mallard nesting in the bow of a lobster boat.

Harold retreated, and his sensitive nature immediately gave him a hard time as he debated what to do. Should he go fishing and perhaps disturb this stowaway by churning his motor seven miles to sea? Should he delay fishing until the ducklings appeared—a maximum matter of four weeks and minus that much income? After the Friendship waterfront gave him good help by dividing down the middle, Harold decided to start *Blossom's* engine and cautiously move to the wharf, to see what happened. He did. He took on fuel and bait, and loaded 50 traps on his stern, ready to go set tomorrow. He put *Blossom* back on mooring, and the duck seemed not to heed anything. Vacant-eyed, as plumed motherhood achieves, she sat. Next Harold went to sea, and she still sat.

We never knew precisely how this finished. She was on her nest one afternoon when Harold moored *Blossom* and came ashore at day's end. The next morning she was gone, and except for one sterile egg on the boards, no evidence of a nest remained. Harold believes someone or something molested her, but I disagree. We had barnyard-domesticated wild mallards for years, and I was convinced she brought off her brood and moved them along overnight.

The best evidence that I was right came a year later, the other day, when Harold came into my workshop to impart, "She's back." Just about the same story. Harold was readying, and was trimming his forward compartment when he engaged the beady eyes of the old girl again. Same place. And with recollections of last year in hand, Harold didn't hesitate. He kept on getting ready, and when he brought *Blossom* to the wharf to get fuel and bait, the duck did as before—she paid no heed and continued to sit.

But this time the program, and the outcome, took a different turn. This season, Harold decided to haul *Blossom* out, scrape her and copper her hull, and paint. This was to be done at a boatyard three miles up Friendship River from the harbor, and after the trip up the river Harold looked, and the duck was right there, serene and confident, showing no concern. "Good girl!"

said Harold. *Blossom* was now fitted into a cradle and the cradle winched up the marine railway. Still the broody mallard attended to her duty and made no never-mind. On the railway, *Blossom* was up by the bow, so the angle of incubation was extreme, but Mother Mallard was not offended and made no complaint. The next day Harold scraped and brushed, and his duck attended to her affairs. But the next morning while Harold was coppering, she waddled aft, jumped to the sternsheet, gave a jaunty quark!!! and took off in search of food—something a broody bird does from time to time, presumably when hungry. She had covered her eggs with the down, and Harold found she still had the 12 eggs he'd last counted a week ago. Harold kept a-painting, and she never came back.

That's it. A year before, *Blossom* had moved about but always come back to the mooring. This year, the hen failed to notice that *Blossom* was ashore, three miles from home. Fishermen at the harbor saw her. She was flying around and around *Blossom's* mooring, now occupied by Harold's skiff, and she was in a tizzy of agitation, and she was quacking and squawking so's to break your heart.

Blossom stayed on the marine railway a little over a week. The unattended eggs cooled down, and Harold properly disposed of them and the nest. Then, shining with new paint, *Blossom* was brought down the river to the harbor and put back on her mooring. Harold was ready for the summer lobstering. Two days later he came into my shop so I could repair a broken handle on a clam hod, and he said, "She's back!"

"The duck?"

"Want to guess what's happened?"

"Started building another nest?"

"Eyah."

1982
Finding My London-by the-Creek

To a State-o'-Mainer brought up to believe in ham-and-eggs, home-fries, cream-tartar biscuits, and blueberry pie, the watercress sandwich appeals only slightly, and is frivolous to boot. I have experienced the watercress sandwich twice; first at the Dorchester in London. In Paris one visits the Louvre, I was told, and in London one goes to the Dorchester for watercress sandwiches. Some day I may return to Paris because of the Louvre. But I have found a better place for watercress sandwiches, and have no plans to revisit London. Come, and we will all the pleasure prove. . . .

Kennebago Lake, far up in the corner of Maine, a smuggler's step from Quebec, is about as good trout water as we have left. For many years the brooks and streams that flow into the lake have been closed to fishing. The idea is that these brooks are nurseries for fingerling trout, and after a happy youth the little darlings move down into the bright lake to entertain the anglers, so Kennebago remains about as fine trout water as we have.

It is even so, and I like to work down the shore from Blanchard Cove to Pyramid Rock and prove the pleasure. I am an equal opportunity angler, but I always pay extra attention to the gurgle where Wilbur Brook comes into the lake. If I approach carefully and adroitly lay my professor on the third circle of that gurgle, my breakfast will run about a foot long, and I have always been partial to Wilbur Brook. It was out of pure curiosity that I forewent my angling one lovely day, left my rod with the canoe, and with goodies in my pack basket walked up the ridge along Wilbur Brook to see what a trout nursery might be like.

The ridge is steep. Wilbur Brook is 1.75 miles long, and in that distance falls over 800 feet. The brook is a series of short cascades, rock to rock and pool to pool, with much tinkle-tinkle under tall hardwood trees. The waterfalls are short enough so a trout can "ladder" them, and here and there in a pool I could see the small fish philandering their childhood and getting ready for the lake. Some of them were not so small. And, as I expected, because it is usual in that region, I came soon upon the beaver dam. The pond was maybe an acre, and the beaver house in the middle was at least a four-family condo. Trout in the pond announced themselves as they rose for mayflies, and jeered at me from their protected situation. Above the beaver pond was a swampy flowage that I had to walk around before I found the brook again.

When I found it, I found, too, a beautiful spot for my nooning. There had been a brow here in the long ago, a place where a lumbering operation stacked logs, and the area had not grown back to timber in the same way as the surrounding woodland. I had a grassy bank with wildflowers, and no sooner had I reclined and opened my pack basket than a cock-o'-the-woods flew in and tore a tree apart. The Auduboners deplore the chainsaw but applaud the pileated woodpecker, but the destructive capacity is about the same. This fellow whacked into the top of a dozy old yellow birch and chips flew all over the place. There's no such entertainment at the Dorchester. Then I walked over to the brook to fill my drinking cup, and made an interesting discovery.

The brook divided, one branch going upstream NE and the other NW, with a huge boulder between. I dipped in the nigh branch, and found my watercress. The stream was clogged with it, extended up as far as I could see. There was none below the big rock. So I found a place where I could stand and look around the big rock, and in the NW branch there was no watercress.

Not a wisp. The sharp, crisp, cold water in my tin cup told the story. The watercress likes cold water. I waded over to run my hand into the NW branch, and the water was nowhere near so cold. I had no thermometer, but I'd guess a difference of ten-fifteen degrees. Within ten-fifteen feet. The two branches mixed their waters at the big boulder, and between there and Kennebago Lake there had been no watercress. I gathered cress and loaded it into my sandwiches, and as I always carry on a conversation with myself at my private picnics, I thought of the Dorchester that noon and affected a Cockney accent.

But think—had I gone up Wilbur Brook on the other side, and missed that cress, there would be only the Dorchester.

1983
Tongs for the Memory

The storage battery in my little garden tractor quit, and I had to lift it out to put in a new one. It's heavy and in a tight place, so I couldn't seem to work my fingers in to get sufficient grip. I don't have one of those straps for lifting batteries. So—I went to my Museum of Awesome Oddities to fetch my old iceman's ice tongs, which neatly snaked the battery up and out. These tongs are not just something for display; they are the tongs I used when I was an iceman back in high school summers and earned a full dollar a day, every day except Tuesdays, Thursdays, and Saturdays. We peddled off an ice cart three days, and then on the others a different crew filled the cold boxes at the markets. That was heavy man's work, and I was only a ten-center. Ten cents was about right for a small icebox at the top of a flight of stairs. So ice tongs will handle a storage battery, and this made me think of two things—Ruel Butler, and the iceman song.

Ruel was never a student, but he knew more practical things than all the rest of us put together. He read slowly and without profit, and he always put two t's in cat. It was in the physics laboratory that his wide knowledge proved his undoing. We had come to electricity, and had fiddled with the Wheatstone Bridge and the machine with a crank that stood our hair on end. The teacher explained how a storage battery works, and Ruel raised his hand to tell her she was mistaken. That's not the how of it, at all, he said. She, her dander up, bawled poor Ruel out for intruding thus in a serious moment, and told him to bear in mind that she was teaching this class and if she wanted to hear from him she would let him know. Crushed, Ruel hung his head, but we heard him mumble that some day she'd start a fire. That teacher was never anybody's favorite—but pupils come and go, teachers stay, and Ruel got a big flunk in physics. You see, Ruel's father had an automobile repair shop, and while I peddled ice and such, Ruel helped in the garage. He swept out and pumped gasoline, and took care of the storage batteries on the charging line. He knew all about storage batteries, but he didn't know enough to keep it to himself. I have always acknowledged a big debt to Ruel, who taught me never to know more than Teacher—as a consequence I had several good grades in subjects where I should have had better.

As to the iceman song—it was on a phonograph record and enjoyed popularity enough so people often sang it as I came upstairs with my ten-cent ice. I can remember some of the words and some of the tune, but that was long ago and I'm hazy in places.

Only us oldsters will remember the iceman. Mechanical refrigeration was well ahead, then, so pond ice was stored in the winter in rambling sheds under sawdust to be brought out in the warm months and distributed about town. What we call a refrigerator was then an ice box or an ice chest—a zinc-lined and insulated cabinet with a lift cover on top, where the ice went, and a door on front for the food space, and a drip pan beneath. More refined customers might have a drain pipe instead of a pan. When a housewife needed more ice she would put the ice card in her window, and we boys on the cart would spot it and respond. Now and then we would lug a piece of ice, by the tongs, up two flights of stairs to have the lady say, "Oh, I didn't want ice today!"

"Your card is up."

"Sorry—I forgot to take it down from last time."

The iceman, if the lady did want ice, would lift the top cover to reveal numerous perishables snuggling against the remnant from last time—a cucumber, tomatoes, smelts, leftover corned beef hash, a wedge of cheese, all put against the ice because the food area was full. He removed these, took out the remnant, put in the new ice, and then chipped the remnant so it would fit back. "Be sure to put the food back!" she would call, and then, "And while you're there, why don't you dump the pan for me?" All for ten cents.

The ice-man song went something like this:

> It's nice today, lady,
> Any ice today lady?
> > How about a piece of ice today?
> It's only a quarter,
> You know that you ought-ter,
> > Hurry up before it melts away!
> > Yes ma'am, no ma'am, not on your linole-am,
> > No ma'am, yes ma'am, giddy-up Napole-an—
> > Your heart is on a nice man,
> > And so is your old ice man,
> Oh, lady, be good to me!

All of eighteen then, I didn't mind if somebody greeted me thus as I struggled up the steps with a ten-cent piece.

Author's Note: Soon after this essay appeared in the *Christian Science Monitor*, I received a letter from Martha Cheney of Lincoln, California, who sent along a tape of herself singing the iceman song. The dear lady has a good voice, and she corrected my memory in a couple of places. Mrs. Cheney's rendition of this song is now deposited in the special collections of the Bowdoin College libraries as a memorial to the Iceman. On the tape, Mrs. Cheney says she recalls the song from her childhood.

1983
Take It from a Walking Boss

R ight-o, I'll take care of it first thing in the morning," I responded, and then I added, "Father." Since I was responding to my wife, who had reminded me of something to do, the additional "Father" seemed odd to the gentleman who was with us, and he looked up to ask, "Father?"

It's a lovely story.

Del Bates, who was a lifetime lumber-camp clerk for Great Northern Paper Company, used to tell the story to help young men who took their work too seriously. Del himself maintained serenity and kept his cool no matter how complicated and arduous his chores became, and he explained that he learned to be like that from his father.

His father was a walking boss. In those days chopping camps were usually closer together than in our days of heavy machinery, and an overseer could manage several operations at once by moving about. Probably Del's father didn't walk from camp to camp, but rode in a set-over pung behind a high-stepping horse. The set-over pung was a Maine woods device, permitting a single horse to travel over a logging road otherwise used by teams. The horse could walk to one side, instead of up in the middle where there was no track.

I met Del and heard his story some 20 years ago when he was "cock-o'-the-woods" in his cock-shop (clerk's office) at Scott Brook Lumber Camp. I was much taken with Del at once because over his office flew a Jolly Roger with skull and crossbones—an unusual ensign to come upon in that remote wilderness.

Del had many yarns about his father, who must have been a remarkable man. He said his father made no restrictions on Saturday night pleasures, and he and his brothers were free to choose, but there was a house rule that the last boy to bed Saturday night had to milk the cows Sunday morning. His brothers, in time, found things to do, but his father felt Del had the makings of a fine camp clerk and he steered him accordingly. Afterward, Del studied at an accounting school in Boston, and readily found a place with Great Northern. One of Northern's managers told me once, "If I had to set up a camp from scratch, and could have my choice of all our company clerks—I'd take Del."

So before Del went away to school, his father took him into the woods with him now and then to learn about lumber camps and the men who worked in them, and he would give Del small chores to do in the way of "bean counting." A bean counter in woods lingo is a clerk—a man who keeps inventory and will know if the commissary has enough beans on hand. Del said he liked the prospects and tried hard to please his father.

Then one afternoon they came to the Six-Mile Camp on Masardis Surplus, and it so happened that the spare bunk, reserved for the walking boss, was the only available bed. Del and his father had to sleep in it. Del was not yet in high school, so he wasn't all that big, but it was still tight quarters. The crew turned in, the ram-pasture quieted down, and the snoring began. I can hear Del now:

"Father went right to sleep, and after a time I did, too. But boy-fashion I was wanting to please the old man, so in my sleep I suppose I got to pondering on the things he'd set me to do, and I came up fitful and restless. I must have churned a good deal, because two-three times he'd poke me and say, 'Stiddy, stiddy!' But I kept on squirming, and finally in my dreams I must have got things squared away, because all at once I sat up in the bunk, still sound asleep, and I calls out, 'Yes, Father! I'll take care of that first thing in the morning!'

"But my father had had enough by then and he had a different idea. 'Nothing doing!' he yells back so he woke every man in the camp; 'you go take care of it right now!'

"And he kicked me out of bed. I sat up in a chair until daybreak, the longest night of my life. And my father never said a word about kicking me out of bed, but the next morning as we rode along, he said, 'Son, never take your work to bed. Leave it on your desk. Most important thing of all is a night's sleep.' "

1984
By the Light of the Silvery Spoon

These good-garden sprays that control bugs and blight are measured by tablespoons, so many to a gallon of water, and I have just the right thing—a tablespoon. I hadn't been giving my tablespoon a thought, but I was mixing a dollop for the squash the other morning when Jim happened by and wanted to know. My tablespoon, you see, is sterling silver, and Jim was aware what has happened to silver of late. Jim says I should lock it up at night. Perhaps I should, but it belongs on the high shelf where my several cans are out of reach. My spoon goes back to my grandfather's time when he was burned out—lost house and barn and all—and had to start over.

After the embers and ashes cooled, he moved on a wood-chopper's tar-paper shanty he found somewhere, got out saw-logs for a bungalow and barn, and began scouring the countryside to find things he needed. Gramp was a trader, and he got a good many things at the auctions about the area. In those days, right after the World War, the country auctions had not become social gatherings for curio collectors or mother lode for antique dealers. They were just sales meant for the neighborhood, usually the last gasp of a family that had run out—offerings of goods and chattels, house and land, all sales final, the accumulation of a lifetime. People from Connecticut and New Jersey hadn't begun to come up to Maine to pay $150 for a chair that was easy worth 35 cents. When they did begin to come, they were looked upon as intruders, spoiling the whole purpose of a good auction. That summer my grandfather did buy 12 dining-room chairs—how much apiece and take the lot?—for 25 cents apiece. He needed only four, so he sold the others at a dollar each, making a profit, so to speak, on four chairs that cost him nothing. Grandfather was a shrewd trader.

Well, one Saturday the old Bingham place on the Brook Road was sold off, lock, stock, and barrel, and Grandfather expected there would be many things he could use. He attended with his horse and wagon and looked the items over before the sale began. He liked the looks of a mowing machine and a separator, and thought he might bid on the vise for heading apple barrels. He had the horse tied to a tree on the lawn, with some hay thrown down, and he sat on the wagon seat to wait the exercises. Squire Chet Longway was the auctioneer, and he was a good one. About midway of the sale two men brought on an ancient trunk—one of those steamer trunks with rounded lid and iron bands. The way they walked, the trunk seemed heavy. Squire Longway had a whispered conference with the two men, who were his helpers, and all three shook their heads. When Chet turned back to the crowd he said, "Now, folks, this here trunk has got to be sold unopened and sight unseen. No key. The trunk has been in the Bingham attic for many, many years and nobody knows what become of the key. Nobody knows what's inside. There's something, but who knows what? So I'm offering this as a mystery box, and how much am I offered?"

Grandfather shouted; "Fifty cents!" Chet ignored him. Again, Grandfather shouted, "Fifty cents!" and Chet ignored him again. So Grandfather kept shouting his 50 cents and Chet kept ignoring him until somebody down front said, "Hey, Chet, you got a bid up back—you gone deef?" Chet said, "I heard that minnow bid and it's an insult to public intelligence. Regardless of what's inside, the trunk alone is worth five dollars. Now, who'll give me an honest bid and start things off at five dollars?" Grandfather shouted, "Fifty cents!" and the crowd, amused, decided to let him buy. The only bid was the 50 cents. The men put the trunk in Gramp's wagon, and when he got home he looked through boxes and pails from numerous previous auctions, and found a key that opened the trunk.

It had quite a few things in it, so it was well worth the 50 cents' investment, and Grandfather was pleased. And it seems somewhere back in the Bingham family there had been a renegade who liked to steal spoons from hotels and restaurants. Gramp found about a peck of spoons. Mostly they were plated, but the tablespoon from Bailey, Banks & Biddle was coin silver and my grandfather used it the rest of his days to mix garden stuff. Then my dad used it, and now I use it. It is not for sale, and no matter what silver decides to do, I'm going to keep it.

1985
Treasured Up Forever

That same schoolmarm who taught me to "dangle participles in secret and split infinitives out behind the barn," the one who wept at "quick glance" and "most perfect," and insisted above is an adverb, was the same who perfected our knowledge that the Smithsonian is an institution. Which is why I wince at all the times it turns out to be an institute. Well, after all these years I am a benefactor and the Smithsonian Institution has thanked me for my most generous deposit. It's the institution's own fault, in a way. It has a philatelic collection, including items from the Railway Postal Service, and a recent exhibition of old RPO stuff was mentioned in the papers. RPO—that was a Railway Post Office, which long since joined the dodo and responsible journalism and breakfast oatmeal as lost causes.

My Dad was a railway postal clerk—a real RPC—and rode several million miles standing up back and forth between Boston and Bangor, Maine, back in the 2-cent days. His RPO was "Vanceboro and Boston," and while the train kept on going to Halifax, he got off at Bangor to rest a few minutes before returning to Boston. Eastbound he sorted letters for all the towns in Maine and the Provinces, and westbound he became the "city clerk" and sorted Boston. The mail car, always next behind the locomotive, was actually a rolling post office, with a mail slot for platform use at stations, postage stamps for sale, and its own cancellation stamp. Instead of a postmaster, it had a "clerk in charge."

So that's all gone, and prices have mounted, and the Smithsonian Institution considers the Railway Mail Service in museum condition. As the son of an RPC, I had certain contacts with Dad's career, but the only thing I inherited was the rubber stamp with which he marked his "facing slips."

When he pulled a handful of sorted letters from a pigeonhole in his case, he would tie them with a cheap jute string now superseded by rubber bands, and on the face of each package he would put a slip that showed the destination. Much of that was esoteric with the mail service, but a good many slips would say Bangor, Millinocket, Lincoln, and so on, town by town. Westbound, for Boston, he had slips for Grove Hall, Astor Street

Station, Newspapers, Banks, and all the carrier routes. Also for connecting trains—the "Springer" for Springfield and the "Shore Line" for the New Haven. All this was known as "separation" and "distribution." Dad took an examination one time on 30,000 Boston firm names and came home dispirited because he scored only 99.92 percent correct.

Each of every postal clerk's facing slips had to be stamped for identification—if a mistake occurred in distribution, the culprit could be identified for demerit marks. Since Dad worked "six-and-eight" and was gone a week each tour, he had to take a whopping supply of these facing slips in his grip. In my turn, it was my job to sit at a table on Sunday afternoons and thump-thump-thump that rubber stamp on hundreds and thousands of facing slips, until the house rattled to the rafters. One slip for every package of mail he would "stick" (sort) for all of Maine, New Brunswick, Nova Scotia, Prince Edward Island, part of Quebec, and all of Boston City. Plus spares and extras, and a good many that said "All for firm on face."

You want to know something? Before I was 15 I knew more about the U.S. postal service than all the postmasters general from Frank Hitchcock to Jim Farley. After that, Dad turned to my brother and two sisters, and in our combined time we thumped a good number of his rubber stamps until they no longer gave off his name, but left merely a blur. The rubber stamp that survived his retirement was left with the date of his last "run," in October of 1941. It reads, "Vanceboro & Boston RPO (SD) Tr. 8. Franklin F. Gould." SD means southern division.

Most of his RPO gear had to be "turned in," his badge, his "scheme book" (for train schedules and mail connections), and the monstrous great .45 revolver he was supposed to wear at all times to protect the mails but never did. But the rubber stamp for facing slips was his, and he brought it home. At some time or other it got among my keepsakes, and there it was in the back end of the second drawer down when I read about the Railway

Postal Service exhibition of the Smithsonian Institution. Treasured up forever, Dad's rubber stamp for RPO facing slips just happened to make me think of that schoolmarm.

1986
In for a Good Kneading

John Bartlett uses a whole column of type to list all his quotations about bread, but he has only one reference to John the Baptist. Is this not a good thing to know? Bread has sustained itself and us from forgotten times, except that nobody much outside of a factory makes any nowadays, and perhaps extinction looms since you can't have John the Baptists unless you bake bread. (I can't consider the factory bread of commerce now rampant in the land, even if its palatability has been raised to that of a paper towel. To make John the Baptists, you need bread *dough!* So home-baked bread is in context.)

At least once a week I am asked to "bring up" the bread mixer, emblem of a happy home, and nobody has ever told me why a kitchen item that gets used weekly must be stored down cellar with the jars of pickles and the water pump. But I bring it up gladly and after the bread is riz I take it back down. And for every carry up and down I get my just reward of John the Baptists—proving I will do well to ask no foolish questions.

A John the Baptist is a little bread cake made by frying a dollop of dough in a spider. I have no idea why it is so called. If such a dainty were not called a John the Baptist, it would probably be called fried bread dough. And a John the Baptist certainly frustrates the demands of the emancipated woman who has allowed the bread factories to take over her domestic pleasures.

We unspeakable gents left the baking of bread to her, with con-comitant privilege of being loved by eaters of John the Baptists, and lo—we don't get any. The torch was not held high and equal rights took over. Honestly, now—when did you last have a John the Baptist?

I had four this morning, and I am full of my subject. Mix the dough for a batch of bread—our mixer does four loaves at a time and the John the Baptists. Cast the dough on the breadboard (grandmothers always called this "casting" dough) and let it rise. Pay heed to time and temperature, and when it has riz, give it a good kneading. Slap it around. Housewives who have not loved their families this way in a blue moon may tire easily, but keep at it—it's worthwhile. Do it right.

Now let the browbeaten dough catch a breath and rise again, and cuff it back a second time. It is now ready to be cut for loaves and put in the pans to rise again before baking. But you will take away enough for a pan of John the Baptists and make them ready before they rise the third time.

Pat the dough for the John the Baptists so it's not quite an inch thick. You can roll it if you wish. Then with a biscuit cutter you do just-'s-if you were making cookies or doughnuts (but no doughnut holes!) and lay things by until the frypan is ready. Bacon fat does all right, and in a pinch you can use butter.

Now comes the secret—and every good recipe has at least one. Don't have the frypan too hot, because the dough for these John the Baptists has riz only twice, and the yeast action is delayed. Have the frypan just hot enough so the John the Baptists will puff a mite before they begin to cook. Then, when they're ready, turn the heat up (or move the pan to the front of the stove!) for a bit of a brown crust. It is well to synchronize this with the assembly of the family at table, since John the Baptists and families should always approach each other just right.

Some may liken the John the Baptist to an English muffin, which we can pass over without comment at this time. They do split up the middle, and then comes a widely divided opinion as to how a John the Baptist should be eaten. The various differ-

ences all start, however, with butter. Then some take marma-
lade, some quince jelly, some raspberry jam, and apple sauce is
all right. A comb of honey or a drench of maple syrup? There's
nothing wrong with molasses, either. It's pretty hard to spoil a
John the Baptist when it's made with care and comes hot.

I should add, I suppose, that the full column of type with
which "Bartlett's Familiar Quotations" covers bread has to do
with bread. The reference to John the Baptist is about something else.

1987
Clang! Clang! Clang!

With 10 cakes aflame with 10 candles apiece, each borne
by one of the 10 grandchildren, Mother took notice of
her 100th birthday anniversary surrounded by her clan and
friends, and a couple of incidents connected with this centennial
transcend the limited interests of those present—incidents worthy of public record and wider acclaim.

Toilichte cendamh, Mathair! (The exclamation point is not necessarily pronounced.)

Born a century ago on Prince Edward Island, my mother
watched the arrival of more progress than graced any other similar period in the history of mankind. Simple comforts and con-
veniences taken for granted now were novel in her time. She
was a woman grown before she saw an electric lamp. Today she
flies but dislikes the tedious automobile ride to the airport, and
she tells about the first time she saw a railway train and an automobile—and a plane. She is alert and keen, a whizz at Scrabble
and the house champ at canasta. Not long ago she remarked

that of all the things she had experienced in her time, she had never had a ride on a fire engine.

So on her 100th birthday the chief of the fire department of West Caldwell, N.J.—where Mutti winters with my younger sister—came around with a couple of engines from the central fire station.

Supported by His Honor the Mayor and the head commissioner, the chief boosted Mom into the cab of the No. 1 hook-and-ladder and hauled her to the place of the big reception. But when Mother was told that she would be thus honored, she looked up to ask, "Will there be horses?"

This is a family esoteric. I have known Mother longer than anybody around (being her first-born) and when I was a tad and came home from school with a new primer, Mother eagerly coached me as I floundered with letters and their words, and this was my introduction to literature. My favorite story in that primer went like this:

> *Clang! Clang! Clang!*
> *What is all this noise a-bout?*
> *See those hor-ses run-ning down*
> > *the street!*
> *Are they run-ning a-way?*
> *No!*
> *They are go-ing to put out a fire.*
> *Clang! Clang! Clang!*

Since that time clang-clang-clang has been a watchword in our family, and Mother's query made great sense to everybody except the brave chief of the fire department in West Caldwell, N.J., who is much too young to remember the three-horse hitch and the furor of a steam fire pumper. Mother bussed him soundly for his gift when he handed her down after the ride and the siren was quiet—she told him it was the best gift of the day.

The other incident that merits public reflection has to do with Her Majesty. Mother received birthday greetings from three or four governors, some congressmen, and so up to President Reagan.

Then, because she was Canadian born, she had a message from the prime minister at Ottawa, and another from the provincial minister at Charlottetown. She was particularly pleased with her message from the Clan MacLeod, of which she was the newest member 100 years ago. (There is never a Scot so Scottish loyal as the one farthest from The Highlands, and one of Mother's grandchildren was piped for a Highland Fling while the cakes were being served.) So things went, and the pile of cards and letters by her seat of honor was bigger than she. And, since the Queen of England is still the Queen of Canada, the topmost message was the traditional greeting from Buckingham Palace.

Now, communications between Her Majesty and her subjects are privileged. We, in the Boston States, wouldn't be so quaint, and if President Reagan pauses to speak to somebody on the street, every reporter and every TV camera pries into what was said and splashes it all around. But not so with the Queen and her commoners, and I respect that and will not tell you what Her Majesty said to my mother on this momentous occasion. The message was in the form of one of these Mailgrams, so it was telephoned to Mother first, and then a printout came later.

The telephone rang.

A dispassionate and disinterested voice began reading the message.

The moment that voice started with "Buckingham Palace," the purpose of the message was understood, and word for word it was taken down in lead pencil on a hastily found brown grocery bag. Thus the centennial greeting of Her Majesty to my mother arrived in the late colonies. The voice on the telephone ran along without the slightest expression and came to the end. The voice said, "The signature is Elizabeth R., last name not spelled out."

1987
There's No Business Like Snow Business

Truth is that the early snows of a rugged Maine winter generally pass us by on the other side. Here at Back River's edge we're too near the ocean, and while folks back a few miles get buried up to the windmill fans, we'll have some rain. Maybe ice right around the freezing mark, so instead of a plow we need sand and creepers.

Sharing with us in this late start of snow are the Joe Bushes, who live down-harbor and two necks over, and Joe is the man who once bought two truckloads of snow, proving that if you live in Maine and don't have enough, you can always get some delivered. Joe lived up in the town of Dexter before he moved to Muscongus Bay—Dexter being up in the approaches to Moosehead Lake where winter sometimes lasts right into the next fall. Joe owned a store on the Dexter main street.

This store had a lunch counter, and Joe employed a clerk who came early and served breakfasts, so when Joe arrived the place was already in business. And one morning in the deepest of Dexter December doldrums, Joe arrived to find several town trucks parked out front, each loaded with snow. The crew had spent all night clearing the business section after a storm, and now the drivers were having breakfast. Everybody spoke chummily as Joe came in, stomping his boots, and then Joe made a tactical error which we must charge off as amusing Dexter whimsy.

Joe said, "What-cha charging today for a load of snow?"

With no hesitation whatever, one driver, geared to said Dexter whimsy, said, "Fifty cents a load—how many loads you want?"

Joe said he'd take a couple of loads.

And right away he knew full well whimsy had struck him out. He knew he'd said altogether too much. The trucks were loaded and ready. But Joe was lucky, because the truck driver also went just that much too far.

The truck driver said, "I'll set you down—when do you want delivery?"

So Joe was off the hook. He said, "Make it the 25th of May." Even in Dexter, which feels closer to the North Pole than it is, this would be a safe date. Even if snow did fall that late, it would be a "robin snow" and wouldn't last long enough to scrape some up.

So the Dexter winter wore along, and every time it snowed the trucks would work all night and in the morning the drivers would be there for snacks, and as usual not only in Dexter, no further remarks were cast regarding the price and availability of snow. Joe hoped, but with suitable Dexter reservations, that the matter was forgotten.

Spring was less reluctant than usual that year. A couple of rainstorms took the snow down early, and the ice went out of Wassookeag Lake 10 days before the average. Lawns leaped into exuberance and crocuses burst with thunderous din. One man brought blossoms from his green pea vines to be put in the window of the *Dexter Gazette*. Unseasonable salubrity lifted all spirits. So Joe was unready when he came down to the store on the 25th of May and found two huge highway department trucks out front with temporary sideboards, nice snow mounded above the sideboards. The drivers were in the store, having their cereal, hungry after their long night drive into the uttermost townships to fetch their loads from the north side of Mt. Katahdin, where Boy Scouts can have snowball fights on the hottest of August days. Joe could see that a plan was afoot to dump this lovely snow on the doorstep of his store.

Joe made the customary greeting on his way to his desk, and he wrote out a check for one dollar, which he handed to the truck drivers without a word. And Joe wasn't at all astonished to find that the Dexter correspondent of the *Bangor Daily News* had been alerted and was waiting with camera and notebook. The next morning the transaction had nearly a full page.

Which is all right, and proves that you never have to go without snow if you want some—but there's a bit more to the story.

Joe had a small powerboat, and that summer he took it on a trailer down to Vinalhaven Island, where he would leave it for weekend purposes. At Rockland he drove his pickup truck, with trailer and boat, onto the ferry, and in due time drove ashore on Vinalhaven. He paused at the island's first filling station to gas up the pickup and to fill some five-gallon cans for the boat. The attendant noticed the home port on the transom of the boat and said, "Dexter, eh?"

"Dexter," said Joe.

"Don't even know where the place is. All I know is some fool up there got his name in the *Bangor Daily* when he paid 50 cents a load for snow."

"You don't say?" said Joe. And that's all he said.

1988
Flags over Oatmeal

Y ou've seen this gentleman on the TV who whales into a bowl of breakfast cereal and says, "It's too good to wait 'til morning!" I disbelieve him, for I haven't seen any breakfast cereal in recent years that has resisted dephlogistication well enough to last the night.

It was a long time ago that I asked the grocer for the kind you cook, and he said, "Well, I guess you could cook any of them if you had a mind to." May I share a last memory of oatmeal that we ate in the evening and saved some for breakfast?

During the war I had a few happy assignments on the *Maine*, an 80-foot diesel patrol boat used by the Maine Department of Sea & Shore Fisheries. From Kittery to Eastport she looked for short lobsters and off-season clams, kept the fishermen honest, and did errands for islanders during predicaments. Then the war struck, and the patrol area belonging to the *Maine* became something of a combat zone and the U.S. Navy took over.

The Navy absorbed the Coast Guard, and all at once there was a big question if Maine had any right to keep a boat in its own waters. Sumner Sewall was governor at the time. He talked to some of the admirals and convinced them Maine had just as much right to keep a navy as the United States did. The *Maine* stayed in service, and not a few of her skirmishes were with the U.S. Navy.

Well, one day a minesweeper manned by hearty jacktars from Minnesota and Nevada came upon the *Maine* cavorting jauntily with the turn of the Fundy tide, and nobody knew just what to do about it. The *Maine* was intercepted, an explanation asked for, and then the radios squawked. The incident ended with Governor Sewall telling the admirals to get their boys off his back.

The master of the *Maine* during the war was chief floating marine warden Clarence Meservey of Brooklin, Maine, who knew every harbor, cove, inlet, and eel rut in 2,500 miles of Down East tidewater, and whose Scots inclinations were not above pulling the leg of established authority. He used to whip out his Maine driver's license when a boarding party of sailors demanded his papers, which seems a mite downright until you learn that several times the sailors didn't know the difference. If they did, he simply excused himself and brought out his state certificate.

The *Maine* "went two," and doubling as cook and engineer was Clayton Simmons of Friendship, who refused entirely, completely, and absolutely to cook any so-and-so oatmeal for Captain Meservey. Clayton hated oatmeal. He could cook all right, and every meal aboard the *Maine* was a Babylonian banquet, so Captain Meservey was happy to overlook this mutinous attitude, and they got along fine. Every afternoon before Clayton got involved with supper, Captain Meservey would call him to take the wheel, and Captain Meservey would descend to the galley to start his pot of porridge.

By the time of World War II, proper all-night oatmeal was gone from our domestic grocery stores, but it was still available in Maritime Canada, where Scots still speak Gaelic, even.

So when the captain needed more oatmeal, he'd schedule an inspection of a sardine factory at Lubec and make a run down that way with the *Maine* to enforce the laws made and provided and get a peck of oatmeal in St. Andrew. On the return trip (to the west'ard!) Cook Clayton would grouse about tripping over the stuff in his galley. I mean oatmeal—not rolled oats—and I mean the kind that cooks and cooks the way it used to. The captain also kept thick farm cream and rich Barbados molasses in inventory—two things all true believers take with oatmeal.

The war was at this stage, then, when I made my first voyage with Captain Meservey and Mr. Simmons. The captain welcomed me on deck and said, "You play cribbage?"

"World's champ!" I said, modestly. He said, "We'll see."

That afternoon we were well off Frenchman Bay when Captain Meservey called Clayton to take the wheel. He had his pot of oatmeal mulling along before he returned, and shortly he brought the *Maine* into a cove and tied her to a vacant spile on a fishing wharf.

Clayton soon served supper, and we were snug for the night. When Clayton cleared the table, the captain brought out the cribbage board, and we fought valiantly game after game—Clayton soon left us and rolled in. Clayton didn't like cribbage, either. Then Captain Meservey fitted a rubber band about the deck of cards and said, "Now, just before bed I like to have a dish of oatmeal."

We had a bowl apiece, and that was the last true oatmeal cereal I saw. It was too good to wait 'til morning, but Captain Meservey had left enough for breakfast. Thus World War II lives in memory.

1989
A Pleasant (Yawn) Match of Field Hockey

N ext to the celebrated free week in Philadelphia, the dreariest thing in the world has got to be a game of women's field hockey. For one thing, there's altogether too much running about for what happens. If they'd cut the size of the field down to the length and breadth of my cucumber patch the excitement might be greatly augmented and some peppy moments might accrue.

But we found a way to inject some hooraw into women's field hockey on a recent Saturday and we feel we've a fine idea for lifting intercollegiate athletics into the fun category. First, you need two granddaughters—sisters. One of these granddaughters needs to matriculate at Wheaton College down in Massachusetts and have a flair at hitting a ball with a stick. The other granddaughter needs the same flair and should enter Bates College here in Maine.

Then you schedule a game between these two colleges and notify the grandparents that they must attend. This game was monotonied at Bates, which is in Lewiston and close enough for doddering old ancestors to get there without public aid.

The teams were warming up as we arrived and parked and amongst the two separate throngs on each end of the field we easily spotted our beloved granddaughters, both wearing the same number—16. We had parked so we could watch the warm-ups and lunch, and now we lunched.

It was a lovely fallish day and we were early enough so we ate without haste, savoring roast beef sandwiches which were a kind of bonus. Well, the marketman had fixed us an oven roast a couple of weeks before, and it turned out to be a cut that had first voted for McKinley and was surly about it ever since. When we told the marketman we were unhappy with him, he said he would make it up to us, and he did. We had enjoyed his makeup the previous Sunday, and were now on the dividends.

The homemade yeast bread and other with-its complemented the excellence of the roast beef, and we were lingering with the cry-baby filled sugar cookies when others of our family arrived. The game commenced shortly.

It was a good game, and every minute seemed an hour. The granddaughters actually played against each other as well as on opposing teams so the excitement was intense. Every few minutes I would wake from my postprandial nap on a lawn chair from home and I would break out into an extensive silence.

I saw no reason to cheer for one side against the other. Wheaton scored first, and then after 167 years Bates scored. This game was made slightly different by a men's soccer game going on over the fence on an adjacent playing field. Now and then the soccer ball would be booted over the fence and the field hockey players didn't seem to know what to do with it. Thus the afternoon pleasantly whiled away.

The game ended 1 to 1. An overtime period was played without any scoring, and then they played a tedious, lingering sudden-death period and everything was still 1 to 1. It was a good way to leave our contest of the sisters.

But then came the fun. The joust was over, animosity could be cast aside, and the two teams exchanged endearments before coming off the field—making a run for some tables that had been set up under campus trees by the doting parents of our two granddaughters. The tables were easy to find—the girls followed their noses upwind to the roasting wieners, the two goalies on behind. There was a pot of beans. There was ample of everything.

And there in the golden afternoon of waning September the Wheaton and the Bates field hockey ladies faced off in a gustatory contest such as I never heard of in other intercollegiate competition. And this one did not have the galloping boredom of the 1-to-1 battle of the sticks. One of the coaches went to replenish her beans at the pot, and turned to announce sadly, "It's empty!" It certainly was—I saw one of the goalies empty it.

The Wheaton team was bused home after the collation—except for No. 16, who stayed to visit her sister, No. 16. The picnic things were packed up, and Marm and I drove home with the thought that we had seen higher education reach a new height of civilized accomplishment.

We had anticipated the grim duty of sitting through the doldrum of a game where prudence would keep us from taking sides, and found we could cheer for the hot dogs without offending either side. If colleges adopt the postgame picnic as policy, granddaughters or not, the future will brighten.

1989
The Triumph of the Lunch-Box Sociable

T he subject is the box-lunch sociable. But this is how it came about: The members of my high school class of 1926 decided to reunionate again, and I told 'em if they'd come to my place I'd buy the lobsters and put on a feed. So they did, and when I went to the wharf to pick up the lobsters, Harlan took my clamhod and went down onto his float.

"Pick me out a dozen good shedders," I said, and Harlan said, "Eyah." When Harlan came back up the ramp, I said, "They look fit for the purpose at hand." Harlan said, "Eyah."

And as I opened my checkbook to pay him, the telephone on the wall rang, and Harlan reached over my shoulder to answer it. "Eyah," he said. When he put the telephone back he said, "Talk about being in the right place at the right time!"

"This is it?" I said.

"Eyah. Phone call just said price of lobsters has gone down 15 cents."

So my Dorothy made blueberry pie and a big, fresh garden salad, and I had sweet corn, and the lobsters were sweet, and the day was beautiful, and midway of the exercises somebody said, "Hey! This is more fun than a box-lunch sociable!"

When you were graduated from high school 63 years ago, it's not much of a strain to remember many things since forgotten. I hadn't thought about a box sociable for a long time, and now as we all had another ear of corn we began, "Remember the time . . . ?"

Each girl would put up a lunch in a box carefully disguised so nobody could guess who, and each boy was expected to bid off a box at auction and share the lunch, and the evening, with the lass whose name he found on a slip of paper after he opened the box.

You took your chances on the lunch, but also on the girl, and sometimes the principal satisfaction was that you were contributing to a worthy cause, since the money paid for the boxes usually went to the library. True, 25 cents made an expensive supper back then, and if a box went as high as a half dollar it was safe to assume the buyer knew full well which girl he was about to get.

The auctioneer at these box sociables had to be witty, and was expected to practice chicanery and deceit. Well, if Neddie was sparking, say, the red-headed Glover girl from The Landing, the auctioneer could hold up a box and imagine he saw a red hair under the ribbon around the box, and he would call, "Aha! Neddie, here's the one you want!"

If Neddie was beguiled and bought that box, he faced two possibilities: (1) he got the red-headed Glover girl from The Landing as he desired, or (2) he was paired with somebody like Mrs. Meehan, who was the mother of 10 children, a chaperone for this sociable in the church vestry, and the piano player for the evening's games.*

True, the mother of 10 children could be expected to provide the best box lunch of all, whereas the red-headed Glover girl specialized in cucumber sandwiches with peanut butter and store-bought cookies.

The girls, in honor-bright honesty, were bound to remain anonymous, but . . . if a young lady wanted her own true love to get her box, a telltale nod when her box went up could speak volumes and her boyfriend would know. But this could back-

---

*Games at box sociables, after supper, were Seven-In-Seven-Out, Winkum, Guess-Who, musical chairs, and sometimes Run-Rabbit-Run.

fire. Suppose your very special dear one were fickle, and decided at the last moment to dine instead with somebody new—then her telltale nod would not be for her box, at all, and you would find yourself eating with Mrs. Meehan.

Several years ago they held a box sociable over on Martin's Point, and since it wasn't for any charity we paired off by drawing names from a hat. I looked at my slip of paper and it said, "Didi." Didi turned out to be an exceptionally comely young matron who was my finest box sociable companion of a long and significant career. I had never encountered such amiability and gustatory competence.

Didi and I, after we found out who each other was, retired to a table in a corner of the room, and while others munched in the manner of box lunches, we banqueted. Didi opened her several baskets and hampers, and began by lighting a perfumed kerosene lamp with paisley shade. We began with soup. She showered me with tasty delights, right through to the peach shortcake. She brought out a bowl and whipped cream right there. And do you know? I haven't seen Didi since, but she lingers vividly in my box sociable lore.

1990
Father Wasn't the Suing Kind

E very time I read that a jury has awarded a fat judgment to somebody who sued a conglomerate, I wonder what my father might have won when he found a carpet tack in his cookie. But my father was not the suing kind. And ours was a happy home where a store-bought cookie was so unusual that Dad picked this one up, looked it all over, and said, "Where'd you get this?" Then he bit into it.

My mother made our cookies. Dad's question was therefore a kind of accusation and eager to keep the record straight my mother responded with an injured tone, "Addie Prosser brought it to sewing circle." The ladies had come to our house that Tuesday to tack a quilt, and each had brought her snack for general purposes. Addie had gone to the store and paid good money for "baker's" cookies. We children knew baker's cookies only by reputation—we never had any at table and never in the pantry. So just then my father let out a yip and picked a carpet tack from between his teeth and stood looking at it in disbelief. "How," he asked, "would a tack get into a cookie?" Tacks and cookies should be poles apart. Mother looked at the tack and shook her head.

In those days any boughten cookie we would see in Maine was made by the Loose-Wiles Biscuit Company, which had a huge brick factory near the railroad tracks in Boston's North End. Anybody who rode the steam cars from Down East into Boston was familiar with the building and the long sign: Loose-Wiles Biscuit Company—The Thousand Window Bakery. There may have been a thousand windows, and the sign tactlessly drew attention to the fact that none of the windows had been washed in decades. Inside, the bakery undoubtedly met all sanitation requirements, but from the train things looked, well, trackside. So his curiosity urged him, and my father wrote a letter to the Loose-Wiles Biscuit Company.

"Sirs: [it said.] My curiosity is piqued by finding a carpet tack in one of your cookies. How could this happen? If you can't give me an explanation, will you accept my suggestion that if you wash your thousand windows the bakers may be better able to see what they're doing. Yours, truly, etc."

A week or so later I came home from school, hove my books on the end table, and went to the henhouse to do my evening

chores and pick up my 4-H Club eggs. I found my father and a
dressed-up young man in the grain room, and my father was
telling the other the essential differences, and relative purposes,
of bran, shorts, and middlings. The young man, wearing the
only necktie our hens ever saw, seemed perplexed and was
most uneasy. My father said, "Oh, here's my son John, he was
there when I bit the cookie." Thus informed, the young man
shook my hand vigorously and said he hoped we might become
warm friends.

That young man was a lawyer who had been sent up from
Boston by the Loose-Wiles people to sweeten my dad and fore-
stall the big lawsuit they fully expected. This was probably good
strategy considering the general disposition of the public, but
Loose-Wiles didn't know my Dad. He wasn't that sort. He loved
everybody, and an attorney for a presumptive adversary was
just another person to know.

About 10 o'clock that morning this chap had arrived, introduced himself, and Dad asked him in to sit. At noon Mother fed
him, and she gave him his first cry-baby cookies. Those are
sugar cookies with raisin filling, or sometimes mincemeat with
walnuts, and Loose-Wiles never heard of them. For fun, now
and then, one cookie in the batch will be filled with red pepper,
and the unlucky child who gets it must go under the table and
be a footstool. The young lawyer was glad to hear about that.

The only mention of anything relating to an impending lawsuit was when Dad asked how a tack got in the batter and the
lawyer said he didn't know, and the subject was dropped. After
lunch Dad asked the lawyer if he'd like to see his peach trees,
and they had reached the henhouse by the time I was home
from school. Dad had given the lawyer a dozen of his beautiful,
brown eggs to take back to Boston. He had also figured that the
lawyer was related to the Potts at South Harpswell. One of the
Potts, Simon, had married Nora Foster, who was a cousin of
ours. Almost anybody was related to my father. There was
never any lawsuit.

When the lawyer got back to Boston he had a case of cookies

sent to my father. Mother used to stick them in our lunch buckets for school, and we gave them all away to the other kids.

1990
Fine Toast Starts with
Honest Bread

Gerald Lewis reported with frostbitten greetings at yule-
tide that things in the northern, uninhabited, townships
of Maine were seemly, and that the adjacent Christmas trees
were standing between 50 and 85 feet. He said he and his
brother have nearly completed the new camp they are building.

A "camp" in the Maine woods is any shelter, simple or magnificent—the Taj Mahal would be a camp if 'twere on Lake Bid-
diekahdahkutt, where the new Lewis camp is.

Gerald said his brother does the carpenter work because he
can't cook. "He can't," said Gerald, "even make toast on the top
of the stove." This opens a magic casement on the wide vista of
intense philosophy, because I was told lately by a clerk in a store
that I couldn't make toast in the latest model pop-up toaster,
which was on sale.

I find I can't, and I can't make toast on the red hot cover of a
wood-burning kitchen range because we eliminated our Kineo
bilingual baker years ago when we embraced the absurd won-
ders of a new age.

Gerald is still joyful in the vicinity of a four-cover, double-
doored, wood-burning Bangor mogul with mitten shelf and
sock rods.

As an electrical toaster, the man told me, it is engineered for store-bought, baker-foundry alleged bread, presliced, and that so long as I insist on homemade stuff I will never get any decent toast. I hadn't figured this out for myself, as I was willing to suppose the toaster factory was incompetent, but as soon as things were explained to me I could see what a simpleton I am.

Home-baked bread, loaded with nourishment and TLC, takes longer to toast, and before it can brown to its desired magnificence the foolish toaster has tripped its automatic doohickey and given a snap, and there is the slice of lukewarm bread fully exposed and looking silly.

Given the same exposure, a slice of store bread is just right—as far as looks go.

If you gave a slice of store bread the same heat and time needed for honest bread, you could patch a canoe with it. So it is.

Without setting brother against brother in this toast to-do, I can tell Gerald he should be patient. It is not all that easy to make good toast on the red hot cover of a Kineo Companion. You have to know what you're doing, as when you play a harp or attempt a panel in the Sistine.

To begin—you never use store bread. It isn't built for it. Drop a preslice of store bread on a hot stove and poof!—like a firecracker. Might's-well use a cedar chip. You need something firmly funded with Robin Hood (or Pillsbury's or Gold Medal) and allowed to rise in the yeast like the Orient sun. (Gerald always adds that it sets behind the vest.)

Cuff it around to give it character and let it bulge over the side of the pans. Slice it with a knife, not a sawmill. Bread—I'm talking about bread. That's where good toast starts.

Gerald needs to be reminded that a maker of honest toast must adjust to the temperature, or color, of the hot stove lid. Experience engenders precision. You come along with a plate of bread and you hold the other hand over the top of the stove and sniff. This gives a two-fold test. You find out if the cover is hot enough, and if you don't smell your sleeve burning you know it isn't too hot. So you know if each side should get $1/32$nd of a second, or $3/64$ths.

Also, if you chance to be on the green end of the breakfast woodpile, you can tell if you need to give the reluctant fire as much as five, or even seven, seconds. Either way, the toast will come out just dandy and you will want to butter it and put it in the oven to stay warm until desired.

I have seen people in high and hoity-toity places lay warm store toast in a little basket and cover it with a doily, a nicety forced on mankind by the passing of the Kineo foundry.

At my house, I make breakfast while my toastmate finds fault and then we swap over for dinner and supper. Lacking a Kineo, I make do with a two-slice popper and a push-down starter and a sliding governor. Left is light; right is dark. But I use home-made bread and my light is barely warm and my dark is just.

The clerk told me I *must* use store bread, but we don't allow it in the house. I can make toast on this heinous device only by running the bread through three cycles and holding down eight extra seconds on the last pop. Hardly a morning but I think about my departed Kineo.

If I can wangle an invitation, I think I'll canoe up next spring and have breakfast at the new camp. I'd be glad to fire up that Kineo baker until the covers are just right, and show Gerald's brother how to make toast.

1990
Good Old-Fashioned Milk Toast

Casper Milquetoast was a character in the cartoons of H. T. Webster—a long-suffering, mild, meek, henpecked man who never complained at the most preposterous abuses, a masculine Patient Griselda.

I never understood why milk toast suggested this sort of person, because I liked milk toast and took all I could get. My mother would make it now and then for the family supper, thus saving on meat and potatoes, and it was delicious. When I left home to tackle college, I didn't get milk toast, and there was a dramatic re-introduction to it at the off-campus restaurant of Louis and Harry one evening while Gilman and I were absorbing atomic information as offered by that first authority, Lucretius.

Louis Zamanis was an Athenian and Argiris (Harry) Argiroulis was from Thessaly; they met for the first time aboard a boat going to Rio. That was a devious way in those days to get to the United States, and after they got to Maine, Harry worked for a time in a shoe factory and Louis barbered.

But when Greek meets Greek, they open a restaurant, and by the time I went to college they had a cozy place with 15 tables. Good food at fair prices, and their combined affability proved successful. The far table next to the kitchen had become a sort of student *Stammtisch*, and this was recognized to the extent that other customers left it to us.

Gilman and I would come early for supper and run over our Latin.

Another customer was Mary Leo, who was the town's police matron. We knew who Mary was, but not officially, and when she came in to sit at the opposite corner table she and we would nod and smile, but otherwise we kept our distances. So as Gilman and I were learning how the atoms swerve, we heard Mary talking to Louis, who had come from the kitchen to take her order.

"What you have, Miz Mary?"

"Oh, I don't know, Louis—what do you think?"

"What you want, you say—I make."

Then we heard Mary say, "You know, Louis, I'd love to have a feed of good, old-fashioned, honest milk toast!"

Louis had never heard of milk toast, but Gilman and I looked at each other, and with common childhood recollections we both realized a feed of good, old-fashioned, honest milk toast would taste some old goo-ood.

"How you make it, tell me," said Louis.

Mary said, "I don't rightly know, Louis. My mother made it, and I just ate it. I never made any."

Gilman and I said, together and alike, "I know how!"

The upshot was that Gilman and I, and Mary and Louis, gathered at the range in the kitchen, and Louis learned to make milk toast.

There isn't much to it, and if you look in a book such as Larousse you will be amused at the verbiage deployed—although the truth is that Larousse talks all around the subject and does not tell how to make simple milk toast.

My mother, of course, never heard the word *roux*, and wouldn't have known what it meant. As for *béchamel*, she never heard that word either, and on the face of it would have dismissed *béchamel* sauce as frivolous amusement for foreign chefs who never had to wash the pots and pans they dirtied. She did know about creamed codfish, but it had no French names that she knew of, and was favored in Nova Scotia on boiled potatoes.

That *roux* and *béchamel* were involved was beyond her control.

Mother started by slicing one or two loaves of her own bread and piling the slices on the shelf over the range. She made her own butter, so she melted enough and stirred in the flour. From that point on, her left hand constantly stirred.

Her right hand would bring down a slice of bread, apply it to the top of the range, and turn it after it seared. There was no electricity involved in my mother's cookery. Think of that!

As toast accumulated, each slice golden beautiful, she added hot milk (from her own gentle Bossie) to her mixture. When a slice of toast was laid into a big vegetable serving dish, she covered it with her hot milk sauce, layer by layer, until she had two or three such dishes full and felt there was enough for 10 or 12 appetites.

Louis and Harry had the only restaurant I know of that offered real milk toast upon order. Louis made it just like my Mom's.

1991
High Cuisine, Lowly Kraut

W here the Inn and the Ilz rivers enlarge the off-blue Danube, in eastern Bavaria, sits the ancient city of Passau, which I chanced to visit on cabbage day. No doubt other places, largely German, observe the same day, but it was Passau where I had my introduction to the sauerkraut event. Every farmer for miles around had brought his harvest of cabbages to market, and the piles obscured the ancient cathedral, spires in the sky. Wholesale and retail, the sale was on, and for the next few days everybody would be shredding the kraut.

Here in Maine, next town to my Friendship, we have a kraut mill of repute, and I think of that day in Passau whenever I pass. A Morse family product, Morse's sauerkraut is as fine as the best in Passau, sold in stores and at the mill, and shipped to some of our better known German-American restaurants. People come for miles, and when Morse offers its new batch every fall we have our own sauerkraut festival so far from Passau.

Our family makes its own. I start the cabbages from seed and plan to grow 25 plants. Every other year, because one batch sees us through, Goodwife shreds and attends the fermentation, and then the kraut bides in Ball jars until we feel the need. To those who praise their roast beef rare with Yorkshire pudding, their pheasant under glass, their lobster thermidor, and such-like paragons of high cuisine, I say only that now and then you can't beat a wallop of kindly sauerkraut with real German potato salad (that's something like Echtedeutscherkartoffelsalat for gracious sakes!), pumpernickel, and a knockwurst gently encouraged with mustard. I like a drop of vinegar on my kraut, but can do without caraway seeds. Some say seeds and some don't, but good kraut doesn't need 'em.

All this at this time of year because my cabbages are ready and the shredding starts. Stand back, folks, and here we go!

Sheila Fowler, ticked off by our local kraut traditions, was telling a comical one the other day. She said her mother, some years back, elected to pass the winter in Florida, and after a few weeks there she wrote home to Maine to say she wasn't altogether taken with the place. The weather was kind, and she had a pleasant cottage, and she'd met some wonderful friends, but it wasn't home and she missed chickadees at the pantry window, and so forth and so on.

This bothered Sheila, because she didn't want her mother unhappy, so she bethought herself of something she might do to put things in Florida in a happier mood. She thought of sauerkraut. Sheila's mother dearly loved a feed of kraut. The Morse mill had just completed its fall run of cabbages, and the finished product was lingering in the great curing barrels, waiting to be broken out for the trade. A good feed of kraut would cheer up her mother!

Sheila accordingly made arrangements, which were somewhat complicated, and a gallon of Morse sauerkraut was made ready in a special container. It would go to Florida by United Parcel Service.

At that time UPS hadn't set up a local agency, and it wasn't easy to dispatch from here. We had an 800 telephone number we could call, and somebody answered in New Hampshire. The next day the friendly delivery boy would stop by. So Sheila called, and her gallon of sauerkraut started for Florida to make Mother happy. But it didn't arrive.

Since it was a chore to make the package ready, and an expense all around, Sheila was anxious, and there was also the consideration that dormant sauerkraut, no matter how carefully it is coddled, may not continue in a melodious condition o'erlong. So Sheila called the 800 number again to make inquiry.

United Parcel Service, proud of its reputation and eager to keep a customer pleased, promised every attention, and the next day a second gallon of Morse's sauerkraut left Maine for Florida.

It didn't arrive. By now Sheila was speaking in very short sentences. United Parcel Service was flustered but polite, and the third, and then the fourth gallon of Morse's finest kraut started for Florida. None arrived.

But Christmas did. On Christmas morning Sheila telephoned to her mother first thing, and cried, "Merry Christmas!" Her mother responded and then said, "Guess what! Yesterday afternoon I got four gallons of Morse's sauerkraut!" Then she said, "What do I do?"

Sheila told me she wasn't ready for that one. She thought a second, and then she said, "Get some knockwurst!"

1992
Natatorial Frolics in a
"Heated" Pool

A nonresident taxpayer paused to bid adieu, and said he was fortunate to acquire a new condofluvium in the Sunny South for the winter, an improvement on previous seasonal accommodations, and it has a heated pool.

I said that was just dandy and wished him a pleasant sojourn. Then I turned my thoughts to my jaunty boyhood, and the heated pool we boys had at Nickerson's Creek (krik). In those impoverished days nobody thought of going south to avoid a Maine winter, and nobody along our Atlantic Coast ever thought of dipping into the ocean. Our Atlantic isn't any colder in the summer than it is in the winter, and if you've been along the Maine beaches and presidential mansions you'll recall the signs that entice the tourists to bide:

SURF BATHING
HOT SHOWERS

That's about the size of it.

Summer ablutions in True's Brook were not too bad. This was a spring-fed stream that came out of Potter's woods and ran about a half mile through True's pasture, so it did get the sun, but it never warmed enough so it didn't support trout. Our Eastern Brookie, *S. frontinalis*, needs cold water to survive, and sometimes a trout would jump for a fly right in the pool where we boys were kicking. That was our unheated pool, and it was fresh water.

Our heated pool on Nickerson's Creek was something else again. Nickerson's was a tidal estuary that rambled through some salt marsh. At low tide it drained out to a trickle of fresh water. Then when the tide served we'd have 10 feet of water in our ol' swimmin' hole.

In March and April, during the runoff of snow water, Nickerson's was one of Maine's best smelt brooks. These little delicacies would come up on a tide in great spawning schools, and a dip net would bring up a peck at a time. Sometimes, without a net, I'd run my hand and arm into the water and feel about to catch a smelt by the tail, and in this way brought home many a breakfast for the family, but my arm would be numb right through June.

That such cold water would ever warm up is hard to believe, but it did.

The tide had to serve in the afternoon, and the sun had to be bright. If the sun warmed the dry banks of the creek all morning, the incoming tide in the afternoon would absorb the heat and fill our pool with tepid water. A night tide and a lowery day didn't do anything for us. So along in late May we'd get a bright morning filled with promise, and coastal boys always knew the time of the tide. It would be the day to go to the Nickerson pool. The only trouble was that we were supposed to be in school that afternoon reciting the prepositions and memorizing the counties of Maine in alphabetical order and naming the principal exports of Central America. But I've always believed that Miss Baker, our teacher, was equally aware that summer pulled at us boys and was not surprised that the afternoon session was feminine. Well—Pudgy Littlehall didn't skip, because he was a student, and neither did Teacher's Pet, Ronald Fotherhall.

Miss Baker, understanding but bound to the formalities, would send one of the girls to the basement with a note for Mr. Foster. Mr. Foster was the school janitor, and after a long winter of stoking the school furnace he was glad for a warm day of idleness and would be sitting in his Morris chair putting in his time. He would receive the note, telling him the names of Miss Baker's absent boys. Mr. Foster was also the town truant officer.

It always happened, and it always happened the same way. Mr. Foster knew very well where to find us. He would come ambling the footpath through the puckerbrush to the brink of our sequestered and heated pool, and he would discover us at our vernal and natatorial frolics. I suppose he would stand a moment to recall his boyhood and envy us. Then in a stern voice he would bespeak us, and 70 years later I can hear him still. "Boys! Which of you ain't in school?"

Then he'd turn away and go back to his Morris chair. Miss Baker, next morning, would smile while we sang "Good morning . . ."

1992
A Boyhood Discovery Worth Remembering

Midwinter meditations entertain me, and just now I was thinking about the time I discovered the ancient settlement of New Vineyard.

True, I did some winter camping, and in the enthusiasms of being 12 and 14 we boys had fun setting up a tent in a snowbank. I made a skiboggan for such outings—a sled with two recycled skis for runners. In those days of white ash skis, nobody kept a pair too long and picking up two odd, or unbroken, skis was easy. I—we—would tie our gear and tent on my skiboggan and snowshoe to the scene of our frolics. This would be on a Saturday, and after a good night's sleep, we'd thaw breakfast and then return.

At this time, since the bloom of youth hath faded, I recall my winter camping trips coolly, but still have fervor about the good times I had afield in the summertime. I discovered the ancient New Vineyard settlement in August, and the event cheers me as memory reenacts the adventure on a midwinter evening with popcorn and a good reading apple at hand.

We have a town in Maine named New Vineyard (population 444; 67 Democrats). But the early settlement of the area was in our adjacent town of Industry, on a stern granite mountain where nobody with any sense would try to live. I had heard the story of the first comers. Weary of the sea, seven families from Martha's Vineyard, an island off Cape Cod, came in caravan to take up seven farms along the mountain, where they'd have a new life far from the raging tide. Much like the sailor in the ancient tale who took an oar and walked inland until somebody asked him what it was.

The seven families "squatted" but later bought their lands. But as the original settlers got over in their books, their children moved away, leaving the old folks until one day nobody lived on the seven farms. The road washed out, and the forests reclaimed the fields. The houses and barns fell apart.

I took a notion, along about 1925 or so, to go to the old settlement to see what remained of a noble intention. I had directions and found it, coming with my pack basket, afoot. I found the cellar holes, and nearby lilac bushes and grapevines and relics of fruit trees. Even spoolbushes. Every home needed spools for winding thread and yarn, and pithwood shrubs had been planted by doorsteps. Cut a piece of the bush, push out the pith, and you have a spool. As with Shelley's Ozymandias, nothing beside remained.

So I had come along that bright August day and found the brook that flowed down from the ridge, and I stopped to lower my basket and admire. I was looking upon one of the sweetest scenes of my lifetime, and I pitched my little tent and stayed right there for three days—making walking trips up to the cellar holes each morning.

The brook was not, at least in August, a raging torrent, but cascaded leisurely from pool to pool. Below each cascade was a granite pool, big enough to swim in, and the series would have suited a summer villa of some old Roman of wealth who wished to impress everybody with his place in the Umbrian Apennines, where he nurtured trout to titillate their feasts. Indeed, as I stood in reverential awe, a trout rose in the second downstream pool, offering a welcome I gladly accepted. I didn't carry a rod on such expeditions, but I had a length of twine and a knife to cut a suitable sapling.

In my midwinter meditation I do not neglect the mosquitoes. Black flies are mostly gone by August, but mosquitoes are less kind. I carried a square of netting to cover my face when I slept, and as soon as my tent was up I made a "smudge." Wet pine needles arranged so their smoke wafts through the tent. It helps. I made out, but the whir of mosquito wings predicted the days of living by a jetport, and lulled me in the smoke under my netting. I was also lulled by a couple of porcupines who pledged their troth, as porcupines do, in the top of yonder pine all night.

It was a beautiful place to tent, and I had some salt pork to handle the trout in my frypan. I think about the place often in my midwinter meditations, along with popcorn aforesaid and some reading apples.

I went once to see the place again, but the road had grown to tall trees. Which is all right, because my excellent memory flourishes on demand.

1992
Fishy Tales from "The Blue Peril"

F or all these many years I've neglected to tell our eager readers of the fish route I used to run to sell seafood to the highlanders.

It was in 1922 that I came into possession of my first motor vehicle, so I was 14 years old and operated illegally. The vehicle was a 1917 Model T Ford, which had no starter, no demountable wheels or rims, no storage battery, no lamps (the bulbs had burned out), and no horn. In those days we had no safety inspection stickers, either.

To obtain this equipage I swapped a good bicycle and two bushels of pickling cucumbers, so I was mercilessly cheated by a gentleman who took advantage of an unsuspecting youngster. I went to Steve Mitchell's hardware store and bought a fisherman's foghorn for 35 cents, giving me a horn which I could pick up and blow at intersections. (That's the one I blew at Tukey's Bridge one time and they lifted the draw.)

The vehicle had been a touring car, but all four mudguards were gone, the take-down top had blown off, and the rear seat had departed because the previous owner transported goats from his barn to pasture and back, a matter of seven miles. Henry Ford never thought of goats.

My father, who was a menace on the highways all his life (I've told how he almost ran down Admiral Dewey and his bride with a milk wagon), admonished me about traffic safety when I came home with this thing, and he said if I ever drove it over 25 miles an hour and didn't kill myself, he would.

So then one May as I meditated in school and waited for the teacher to catch up, the thought of a fish route came into my mind. People back from the shore love fish, and I lived in a waterfront town. I could dig clams myself, and get other things at the wharf. I could buy picked-out crab meat at Tom Moody's place for 30 cents a pound. I built a cold-box in the back-seat space and for advertising purposes painted my Ford a lovely robin's egg blue. The "Blue Peril" was created!

This turned out to be a fine idea, but I made two or three trips into the hinterland before I learned some things. Clams sold well, but were too heavy and took up space. Cod and haddock, and other groundfish, needed display room, and it took time to sell them. I gave up hauling clamshells and took shucked-out clams in pint and half-pint preserve jars. By my third trip I was down to the crab meat and shucked clams.

Gasoline was 13 cents a gallon, and my fish wagon would go 40 and 50 miles on a gallon—more when I coasted downhill. On the front seat beside me I had a weatherproof box for clothing and dry food, my pup tent and oilskins. Perishables were in my iced fish box, and I replenished ice as needed. Every town had an iceman then.

At mealtime and come evening, I'd pause to lunch or pass the night (cemeteries are great!) and as folks were not so possessive in those days, I could pause without asking. If I did ask, I was always received cordially. Many a farmer gave me sweetcorn and cukes, and even fresh milk and eggs. I came to have regular stopping places, and I knew many names. A Mr. Dalrymple once brought me three beautiful brook trout for my supper. I was tenting under his balm o' Gilead tree, so I gave him a box of crab meat.

One woman wanted some steamers, but I said I had clams only in the pint jars—ready shucked. She said "Oh, Dear," that she'd been hankering all week for steamers, and said she wouldn't know how to use shucked clams. So I wrote her my recipe for clam chowder (be sure and use the juice!), and she took a pint of clams. Next week she said she'd shared her chowder with friends, and now she had orders for five jars of clams.

There was a state policeman who always waved, and one day I had a flat tire and he took me on his motorcycle to a place that sold me a used replacement for 35 cents. That cop never asked for my license, which I didn't have yet.

I did that for two profitable and pleasant summers. Some weeks Tom Moody didn't have all the crab meat I wanted, but I could always fill my box with harbor pollock and tinker mackerel. Finally, I went to college and spent every cent I'd earned on the frivolities of culture. My first year tuition was $200, but the next year it went up to $250. That's a lot of fish.